Literary Meaning and Augustan Values

Literary Meaning and Augustan Values

Irvin Ehrenpreis

University Press of Virginia
Charlottesville

THE UNIVERSITY PRESS OF VIRGINIA

First published 1974

ISBN: 0–8139–0564–8
Library of Congress Catalog Card Number: 73–94275
Printed in the United States of America

To Louis Landa

Preface

My attitudes toward scholarship and criticism formed themselves in response to some widespread assumptions about the relation of style to meaning and of literary value to both. I have found the principle that style and meaning are inextricably united to be more manageable in the theory of criticism than in the practise. The principle that the value of a literary work is independent of its truth seems contrary to all our experience of art, if by truth one means not the author's sincerity but the work's consonance with human nature. The habit of ignoring or explaining away the faults of an author, the disposition to treat his *oeuvre* as data, which one may praise and interpret but not blame, seems related to the principle that style is meaning. If the two are identified, and we cannot fault a work for wrong meanings, the role of judgment dwindles miraculously.

My debt to books by Geoffrey Tillotson (*On the Poetry of Pope*), George Williamson (*The Senecan Amble*), and Erich Auerbach (*Mimesis*) will be clear to other admirers of those scholars.

Sections of the long essay "Explicitness in Augustan Literature" have been read before the English Institute (meeting at Harvard University in September 1972) and elsewhere. "Personae" first appeared in *Restoration and Eighteenth-Century Literature: Essays in Honor of Alan Dugald McKillop* (Chicago: University of Chicago Press, © 1963 by William Marsh Rice University). "The Style of Sound" first appeared in *The Augustan Milieu: Essays Presented to Louis A. Landa* (Oxford: © Oxford University Press 1970). "The Cistern and the Fountain" first appeared in *Studies in Criticism and Aesthetics, 1660–1800: Essays in Honor of Samuel Holt Monk* (Minneapolis: University of Minnesota Press, © 1967 by the University of Minnesota). I wish to thank the copyright holders for their permission to include these essays here. "The Styles of *Gulliver's Travels*" was originally read at the University of Pennsylvania (February 1972).

Contents

Part One

Some Theories

I. Explicitness in Augustan Literature

Explicit Meaning and Suggestive Style

Literary and Nonliterary Scholarship

Two principles seem at odds in academic criticism today. One is a strict determination to deal with literature in its own special terms, to exclude biography, psychology, history, and sociology, to exclude all occupations in which literature seems employed as document or in which it does not exist as an object to be contemplated for its own sake. A scholar who adheres to this principle may say a work is good or bad; he may examine its versification; he may expose the design of a narrative plot; he may establish a connection between imagery and structure. But he may not tell us about the author's ancestry, his social class, his emotional obsessions; he may not deal with the sources of a work or its reception; he may not consider the influence of the work on the author's imitators. He may perform none of these tasks unless they affect or reveal the literary elements of style, structure, meaning. According to strict constructionists, all nonliterary study belongs outside the province of the scholar or critic because his duty is judicial, interpretative, or analytical. Biographical information may enter into his pursuits only as it affects the interpretation of a work; sources, only if they appear as deliberate allusions in the work.

The other principle is the common pleasure in literature as a human phenomenon, an interest that finds source-hunting, biography, and the psychology of creation naturally fascinating. Scholars and critics too suffer the elementary impulse to learn about the author and origins of a masterpiece. The scholar willy-nilly enjoys discovering that a line from Pope echoes a line from Dryden. He delights in knowing that a character in a play bears the features of the playwright's mistress. He likes to hear from a historian that a powerful essay exerted a deep influence on political reformers decades after its first publication. Even a strict scholar feels tempted to smuggle back into his researches the very lines that he ought to reject.

A priori the strict principle has much to recommend it. Under its pressure, the replacement of a literary work by its author's life becomes difficult. The reduction of a literary masterpiece to an instrument of politics is impossible. The scholar has to focus his energies on the work itself and not on adventitious circumstance. But how then is he to deal with his common curiosities? The simplest way would be to declare that the extrinsic themes deserve his attention whether or not they belong to the official program. This method has become abnormal. Journalists may write about Byron's sexuality; biographers may examine Johnson's melancholia; wayward critics may search James's novels for evidence of the author's emotional crises. Proper scholars are likely to refrain.

The more correct way is to declare that the material has an important bearing upon the sense or design of the work. One may find Proust's style evasive and blurred in certain scenes, and one may account for the defects by showing that the relationship the novelist deals with in his fiction is based on a quite different sort of relationship in his real experience. One may account for the success of a certain poem by arguing that it gives to the social class of its readers a much-wanted moral vindication. One may argue that the source one has unearthed for a scene in a tragedy reveals an implication that earlier commentators had missed.

But the truth of the matter is that often no deep connection exists between the most gripping, extrinsic information and the inner aspects of a literary work. The early drafts of a poem seldom tell much about the final design that one could not infer from the fair copy. Yet to trace the history of the composition of a masterpiece is to teach us much about the psychology of genius. The reliance of a Restoration playwright upon a French or Spanish source will often add little to our understanding or appreciation of his finished comedy. It may add much to our sense of the multifariousness of creative imagination and the mystery of originality. The annals of the influence of a work cannot alter its innate attributes. But it can give us an idea of the power of literature. These findings, so long as they are rich and exciting, need no justification. Yet in trying to justify them, scholars may distort them. We are told to avoid mere source-hunting. Consequently, when a man discovers a remarkable source for a work, he often disguises the revelation, subordinates it to a supposedly fresh interpretation, and pretends that the excitement of the find belongs to the alteration in meaning—an alteration that may be nugatory.

If I am right, should we not offer more resistance to the strict principle? Should we not agree that what seems naturally fascinating is indeed so, or that we may deal with the "nonliterary" elements of a literary work so long as we produce valuable (not trivial) insights into the nature of literary genius and the history of culture? It seems to me that too many scholars have coated a respectable human motive with specious purposes.

Contrariwise, certain methods of interpretation and analysis have been undeservedly exalted, and this levitation has produced a general respect for insubstantial studies that pretend to deal with meaning, structure, and style. Fragile hypotheses have been treated with reverence, unconvincing interpretations have been received as sound, because their proponents worked within the limits of the strict principle described above. I wish now to consider how such a bias has hurt the study of eighteenth-century literature.

Statement and Suggestion

In literary scholarship, as in all human affairs, admirable intentions can produce unpleasant consequences. The best academic scholarship tries to narrow the space between ourselves and the great writers of the past. This operation must indeed be among the supreme purposes of any learning we acquire, for the degree to which a scholar makes us at home in remote ages is one measure of his accomplishment.

Yet our very eagerness to grow contemporary with the Augustans (my bad name for English writers of the period 1660–1760) is what impels us to misrepresent their civilization. In teaching, in criticism, in scholarship we bring to bear on old masters the taste and methods that satisfy our own generation. By dressing the familiar figures in bright new clothes, we hope to change them into young presences. For modern academic critics, lyric poetry has become the quintessence of literary art. So we apply to plays, novels, epics, and philosophical argument the methods of analysis that belong to the study of short poems; and a disconnected story by Dickens emerges from our shop in a gorgeous coherence of related images. When, as academic critics, we teach undergraduates, we meet direct challenges from their fugitive and cloistered virtue. Students are dissatisfied with tragic mystery and ask us to justify the ways of Shakespeare to men. We respond by discovering faults in Desdemona and distributive justice in the death of Cordelia. I sometimes wonder whether the classroom is not a pernicious influence on scholarship. In order to teach, we must have something to say. Poems however magnificent that offer no obstacle to the understanding or the judgment also give little support to a lively discussion. So we turn Gray's *Elegy* into a series of desperate cruxes and discover golden irony in the leaden mines of Defoe.

Some of these transformations amount to distortions, and I suggest that for our period they begin with a pair of judgments: that explicitness is a distinguishing feature of Augustan literature, and that in literary art, explicitness or statement is inferior to suggestion. Because the classics of the Augustans (from Dryden to Johnson) have been associated with a style of statement, we have felt embarrassed. So we have tried to liberate them from the crippling burden; and in so doing, we have falsified them.

The distinction between statement and suggestion, in criticism of poetry, is very old.[1] But as Maynard Mack has said, it was probably Mark Van Doren who started the vogue of the phrase "poetry of statement."[2] Van Doren applied the phrase to Dryden's genius: "His poetry was the poetry of statement. At his best he wrote without figures, without transforming passion."[3] Reviewing Van Doren's book, T. S. Eliot said, "Dryden's words are precise, they state immensely, but their suggestiveness is often nothing."[4] The phrase "poetry of statement" and its associations soon attached themselves to the poetry of Pope, but they recall Johnson's description of Swift's work: "He pays no court to the passions; he excites neither surprise nor admiration; he always understands himself and his reader always understands him."[5] Picking up the hints of Van Doren and Eliot, E. M. W. Tillyard made a systematic contrast between "poetry of statement" and suggestive poetry in his widely read book *Poetry: Direct and Oblique* (1934). Here he devoted a long chapter to Dryden.

Critics like Eliot and Tillyard seem to believe they have missed nothing important in the meaning of writers labeled poets of statement, although explicitness hardly seems praiseworthy to them. I think no eminent critic, unless he has made a special study of the eighteenth century, feels otherwise. While these men are wrong, their impression does reflect what I believe is a real property of the best work of the Augustans, a faith in explicit meaning, a desire for clarity. Cowley described the new fashion of writing, in his day, as one where "all that is meant is exprest."[6] George Williamson, after quoting Cowley's remark, compares Dryden's translation of Tacitus with an earlier translation and concludes, "The most obvious feature of Dryden's translation is that it is filled out, the ellipses have been filled up; the logical relationships have been more exactly expressed; a more natural order has resulted, though some of his sentences are periodic; his vocabulary is more abstract; in short, the expression is more complete in Dryden, and he is less like Tacitus."[7] The same analysis might be made of Dryden's translation of Persius.

It is because the so-called Augustans seldom trusted allusion or conno-

[1] Cf. Krishna Rayan, *Suggestion and Statement in Poetry* (London: Athlone Press, 1972), pp. 1–51. This book has strongly influenced my argument in the present paper.

[2] "Wit and Poetry and Pope," in *Pope and His Contemporaries: Essays Presented to George Sherburn*, ed. J. L. Clifford and L. A. Landa (Oxford: Clarendon, 1949), p. 20, n. 1.

[3] *The Poetry of John Dryden* (New York: Harcourt, Brace and Howe, 1920), chap. 3, par. 2.

[4] "John Dryden," last par., in *Selected Essays*, new ed. (New York: Harcourt, Brace and World, 1960), p. 273.

[5] "Swift," in *Lives of the Poets*, ed. G. B. Hill (Oxford: Clarendon, 1905), III, 52.

[6] *Essays, Plays and Sundry Verses*, ed. A. R. Waller (Cambridge Univ. Press, 1906), p. 421.

[7] *The Senecan Amble* (London: Faber and Faber, 1951), p. 322, n. 1.

tation, imagery or allegory alone to convey their meaning, because they normally made explicit any doctrine they wished to inculcate, that the fathers of modern criticism could so easily ignore other features of their work. Even those Augustan poems that embody dangerous material—subversive politics, personal satire, irreligion—will often be found to include explicit or discursive passages to orientate the reader and keep him from misunderstanding the argument.[8]

It is also a feature of this literature that the author conceives of himself as illustrating or enhancing his explicit meaning through the resources of his art—through distinct figures of speech, through splendid language and expressive versification. In fact, this feature is one consequence of the desire for clarity, because such a desire implies that the same doctrine can be expressed either clearly or obscurely without essentially changing as doctrine—in other words, that the same meaning can be conveyed in different styles. Dryden in his translation of Virgil's *Georgics* says,

> Nor can I doubt what oil I must bestow,
> To raise my subject from a ground so low:
> And the mean matter which my theme affords,
> T'embellish with magnificence of words.
>
> [III, 453–56]

The conception of style as the frame of meaning or (even worse) as ornament applied to meaning is as monstrous a crime as exists in the jurisprudence of modern criticism. We pledge our allegiance to a principle of organic form that makes style and meaning indivisible.[9] I doubt that Augustan writers would have subscribed to this principle if it had been offered to them; and I am not sure it is the best guide to an appreciation of their work. But even if the principle was sound to begin with, it has been ill used by many critics in the last forty years. Organic form no longer indicates a harmony of conception that allows for freedom and variety of expression. It has come to imply that the deep or true structure of a work of art need not appear on its surface, that a poem which at first hearing sounds disjointed may possess a tight inner shape disclosed by imagery and allusions.

Of course, the modern reader is supposed to find one of his literary pleasures in creating the poem he receives by putting it together as he goes along—the way one makes a model from half-finished parts that may be separated and reassembled at will. Whitman said his reader "must himself or herself construct indeed the poem, argument, history, metaphysical essay—the text furnishing the hints, the clue, the start or

[8] For example, Swift, in *An Epistle to a Lady* and *On Poetry*.

[9] Cf. Murray Krieger, *The New Apologists for Poetry* (Minneapolis: Univ. of Minnesota Press, 1956).

framework."[10] This pleasure was unknown to Augustan writers, who strove to give their readers a finished artifact. But we may, if we wish, reduce their complete poem to something more deliciously tantalizing—a collection of parts.

Suppose a scholar is handling a poem written before the doctrine of organic form was widely accepted, and suppose he nevertheless wishes to demonstrate that this poem exemplifies the doctrine quite as well as Romantic and Symbolist poems; his most dazzling feat will be to reveal in it a structure that seems independent of the explicit meaning or that at points even contradicts it. "Structure" in such an operation comes to denote something at odds with the old idea of a rhetorical skeleton or a narrative plot. Yet this crypto-schema often turns out to be as rigid as the genres and patterns from which it was once supposed to free us.

We may as well admit that the whole modern idea of poetry would have puzzled the Augustans. What most critics prize today is suggestion, allusiveness, implicit meaning. It is not enough that a poem should possess depths of implicaton. It must look dark. It is not enough that a poem should be difficult; it should not even seem easy. But the Augustans liked to conceal difficulty under a show of ease; and they liked suggestion to wear an outer garment of explicit meaning.

I am far from saying that for the modern reader the explicit aspects of any poem have to be the most valuable. They may not even be clear. All words are innately analogical; all speech is ambiguous. In ordinary conversation we try to exclude what seem the irrelevant meanings from our unilinear understanding of a speaker's train of thought, and the mode that encourages such limitation is what I call "explicit." It works toward clarity and gives one the impression (often false) that the writer withholds nothing of importance. On the other hand, there is deliberately connotative, figurative, or suggestive speech. This must still have an explicit or literal component, but that component serves as a pointer to an implicit meaning. It is worth observing that an implicit meaning is not always hard to grasp; it may indeed be clear and easy. Thus the primary implication of a metaphor is often simple, although the vague secondary connotations of its imagery may be complex. Conversely, the explicit passages of a poem may be dull, obscure, or trivial; but in them we are trained to attend to only one of the possible meanings.

In keeping with the supposed principle of organic form some modern scholars give their best energy to the labor of drawing meaning out of what Dryden would have considered the less significant elements of an Augustan poem, viz., the connotations of allusions and images. In doing so, the scholars naturally give small attention to the explicit element, ex-

[10] *Democratic Vistas*, fourth paragraph from the end, in *Complete Poetry and Selected Prose*, ed. E. Holloway (London: Nonesuch, n.d.), pp. 720–21.

cept to assume that it is less explicit than it sounds. In other words, they tend to strip the explicit mode of the very attribute of meaning which they then confer on the other ingredients of the poem. In their eagerness to show that the conception of style as frame or ornament cannot account for the shape of Augustan masterpieces, a few interpreters make it appear that the explicit meaning is not even a fundamental part of the poet's design. The frame thus replaces the picture.

Another characteristic of Augustan poetry also troubles modern taste. Not only has the meaning of such poetry seemed clear. It has often seemed unexciting as well. Satire attacking men in high places may be bold and dangerous. But the moral doctrines on which Augustan satire rests are usually commonplace. Yet the modern critic, especially since the Second World War, likes to single out for praise the kind of doctrine that is either subversive of received opinion or profoundly original. It is hard to praise the explicit doctrine of Augustan poems for boldness, originality, profundity, or subtlety when the poet claims in his work to teach familiar doctrines and to make them fresh through his presentation.

Some friends of Augustan writing have tried over the past thirty years to interest modern readers in that literature by showing how it can satisfy the modern taste. They have dwelled on the allusiveness, the indirection, the subversiveness of the authors. In poems that sound conventional they have heard iconoclasm. In plays that seem decadent they have found moral health. Poems that look rambling have been called in and issued with elegant forms.

To accomplish these ends, the scholars have generally discounted clarity or ease of style, and what one finds in many reinterpretations of Augustan literature is really a flight from explicit meaning. At its least adventurous and most persuasive this flight represents a desire to enlarge a literary work, to give it a moral or intellectual setting that must enrich its suggestiveness and make it appear not so different in ultimate effect from the haunting, evocative literature to which it is opposed by critics like Van Doren and Eliot. So one may fly from the text to literary echoes and allusions that set it against a rich, wide background. One may then multiply and sort these allusions to produce a systematic parallel between the work itself and an earlier masterpiece such as the *Aeneid* or *Paradise Lost*. The work then becomes an instance of what could be called "parallel poetry." One may also fly not to literary antecedents but to traditional doctrines—religious, philosophical, political—which the allusions imply, and one may then argue that the work belongs to a different line of thought from the one scholars have usually attached it to. One may elevate literal expressions into symbols and discover allegorical meanings where earlier readers have missed them, or one may treat the air of explicitness as a deliberate mockery, trade the simple meanings for indirections, and read ironically a work that had always appeared straightforward. These are some paths that scholars have made to lead modern readers away from old interpretations, and I shall now try to review the dangers they involve.

The Flight from Explicit Meaning

Echoes and Allusions

When the critic merely provides a background for a passage, he does recognize a poem's explicit meaning. But he tries to show that while this may seem declarative and commonplace, it is in fact alive with suggestion. He does so by linking the work to traditions and allusions that modern readers have lost sight of. What sounds shallow today, says the scholar, had rich reverberations in its own time. So he demonstrates that the theme of a poem evokes intellectual principles and moral ideas long and widely held by a great line of poets, philosophers, or theologians. Among such doctrines, themes, or *topoi* are the chain of being, the value of the contemplative life, *concordia discors*, the golden mean. Sometimes they are related through a religious motif like the doctrine of atonement. One wonders where students of seventeenth-century poetry would be without the Fall of Man, a concept better known to students of the novel as the Rise of the Middle Class.

I should like to make some distinctions here. One is between the origin of a poem and its meaning. It is a valuable and fascinating job of research to discover what forces worked upon the imagination of a genius while he was creating a great poem. But such biographical and genetic insights do not reveal the depth or the meaning of the poem unless the poem invites us to think of them. Even if the poem does in itself evoke ancient traditions, while those may indeed give the poem resonance they cannot by that effect make its meaning either profound or daring, at least to the live reader. No amount of resonance can give sonority to the Golden Mean. Besides, the scholar who validates the argument of a poem by showing that its doctrines were widely accepted by a long line of deep thinkers may put himself in an awkward position if those doctrines appear shallow. He is implicitly saying, They are not shallow; they are commonplace.

Anyhow, the traffic moves two ways. Suppose one winces at the heaviness of some poet's moralizing aphorism. To defend it, one may plead that the aphorism summons up remembrance of past sentiments on the same theme and thus sets off a rippling series of echoes taking us back from Erasmus to the *Greek Anthology*. I reply, maybe these exquisite reverberations did charm the very few original readers of the poem who had so much literature in their heads; but even to them, just as to the modern reader with or without those reverberations, the explicit statement remains present. It is never used up by the suggestions it evokes. The echoes return one to the aphorism; they envelop that; it is their pearl; and in it we confront what is immovable—a heavy piece of aphoristic morality.

In his studies of Pope's poetry, Maynard Mack sometimes implies that he is enhancing the literary value of a work when he is in a most rewarding way disclosing its origins. Professor Mack observes that Pope in a few lines of the *Epistle to Cobham* may echo Cowley's paraphrase of a famous passage from Virgil's *Georgics*, celebrating the farmer's life. "If so," says Professor Mack, "the Virgilian passage masses behind Pope's contrast of court and country the most authoritative of all literary precedents."[11] Now I am puzzled what to make of this. The lines in Pope's poem—

> In life's low vale the soil the virtues like,
> They please as beauties, here as wonders strike—
> [*To Cobham*, ll. 143–44]

are deeply ironical and are framed in an elaborate conceit of Pope's own workmanship. Nothing in the lines invites us to look for literary allusions. Professor Mack observes meticulously that Pope was not deliberately alluding to Virgil or Cowley. Such a passage, he says, shows "at the most reminiscence, not allusion" (p. 85). But the fact remains that the passage is less enriched than confused if one brings in Virgil.

Pope here set the difficulty of being virtuous at court against the ease of being virtuous in an obscure life; he does not contrast city and country. Virgil compares the serenity of the philosopher with that of the farmer and says his own first wish is to understand astronomy and other natural sciences, but if he cannot do so much, he would like to live a country life. It is true, as Victorian editors pointed out, that Pope probably echoes Cowley here. Yet as it happens, he may also be echoing a passage from a comedy by Dryden in which the hero operatically prefers cottages to courts (*Marriage à-la-Mode* II.i.439–47). It seems to me that the more specifically we recall the antecedents of Pope's lines, the more remote the intrinsic, witty art of those lines becomes.

[11] *The Garden and the City* (Univ. of Toronto Press, 1969), p. 83. The line by Cowley (from the translation "out of Virgil," l. 47, in essay no. 4, "Of Agriculture") that Pope echoed does not in fact belong to Virgil's praise of the farmer's life as such (*Georgics* II. 458–74) but to a neighboring passage. Any reader making Professor Mack's connection, therefore, would have to identify Pope's line as derived from Cowley's and would then have to move back from the corresponding line in Virgil (*Georgics* II.485) to the earlier lines.

Of course, we do have to keep in mind a vague tradition of opposing rural retirement to courtly ambition, but the lines themselves evoke that. Of course, it is fascinating to learn how Pope may have based his own poetry on that of others; but if allusions and echoes do not seem deliberately employed in a poem, they can hardly be said to enrich its meaning. I wonder what we gain by diverting a reader from the text to a reminiscence. After all, one never knows how many echoes one has failed to hear.

Scholars who trace allusions sometimes take it for granted that the more precise they can make a reference, the more richly it will enhance the value of a poem. There is a paradox here. Connotation is what one usually wants; one values the precise allusion for its suggestive power. Yet the more general an implication becomes, the less one need pin it to a particular allusion, simply because the context supplies so much of the meaning; the connotation is usually present to begin with, before one has traced the allusion. And the more precise the allusion becomes, the less neatly it fits its context; the more likely it is to beat up awkward references.

In another subtle and scrupulous argument Professor Mack declares that toward the end of Pope's *Epistle to Bathurst* the author deliberately alludes to an ode of Horace. To put the case briefly, Professor Mack says first that Pope's poem shows so many clusters of thematic parallels to Horace's ode that anyone familiar with the Latin lines would think of them when he read the English. Within this context Professor Mack believes that a couplet from the *Epistle to Bathurst*—

> 'Till all the Dæmon makes his full descent
> In one abundant show'r of Cent. per Cent.—
>
> [ll. 371–72]

must be a witty allusion to the myth of Danaë. Since the ode by Horace opens with a peculiar interpretation of the myth, and since Pope implies the same interpretation, Professor Mack concludes that the English poet here "directs our attention squarely" to the Latin ode (p. 88).

I wonder how demonstrative such reasoning is. The themes common to Horace's ode and Pope's epistle also pervade the satires of Persius, nos. III, V, and VI (not to mention other works that deal with the power of gold);[12] and Persius was a favorite of Pope's.[13] The couplet that reminded Professor Mack of Jove's descent on Danaë reminds me of

[12] See especially Dryden's translation of Persius for language anticipating that of Pope's epistle. In Satire III the anecdote of the sick man is used much as Pope used the fable of Balaam.

[13] Austin Warren, *Alexander Pope as Critic and Humanist* (Princeton Univ. Press, 1929), p. 200; Pope, *Correspondence*, ed. George Sherburn (Oxford: Clarendon, 1956), I, 99 and II, 231.

Apollo's descent on the sibyl in the *Aeneid*.[14] Even if one agrees with Professor Mack that this couplet alludes to the myth of Danaë, it so happens that precisely the version of the myth chosen by Horace appears in an epigram of Paulus Silentiarius (*Greek Anthology* V.217), a poet whom Pope echoed elsewhere.[15] Horace? Persius? Virgil? Paulus Silentiarius? With so many vibrations shaking the air, I doubt that even Dr. Bentley, reading Pope's line "In one abundant show'r of Cent. per Cent." would have murmured to himself, "Ah, Horace!" and recalled the opening stanza of *Odes* III.xvi.[16]

The section of the *Epistle to Bathurst* to which the couplet in question belongs is the tale of Sir Balaam. This is a heavy-handed, unconvincing fable preaching the hollowest morality. Its lesson seems to be that people who by evil devices get rich quickly will come to a bad end. I'm not sure how this doctrine would be enhanced by an allusion to Horace's ode, in which the poet says he lengthens his purse by contracting his desires. But even with Horace's support the doctrine would remain hollow. Allusion as such may decorate, handsomely; it cannot deepen.[17]

I do not insist that mine is the one true interpretation of the fable of Sir Balaam, or that the moral of the fable is simple, or that the moral is even a valuable part of the poem. But I do insist that whatever the primary meaning of the fable may be, an allusion to a literary source will neither establish it nor give it moral validity. One must tie any allusion to one's own interpretation of the poem's doctrine; and it would be a miracle-worker who could reconcile allusions to an ode of Horace, the Book of Numbers, the Book of Job, and Thomas Pitt (all perhaps present in the

[14] Compare the language of Dryden's translation of the *Aeneid* VI.78–87, 120–25, with that of Pope's *Bathurst*, ll. 371–74. (Dryden's line 117—which occurs between the passages I have just indicated—was echoed by Pope in *Bathurst*, ll. 75–77.) Or else, combining the idea of rain with sexual possession, and anticipating Pope's language, there is Dryden's translation of Virgil *Georgics* II.440–41: "For then almighty Jove descends, and pours / Into his buxom bride his fruitful show'rs." For other anticipations of Pope's language by Dryden, see the translations of Virgil *Pastorals* VII.83:"Jove descends in show'rs of kindly rain"; Persius II.91; and Ovid *Elegies* II.xix; also *Annus Mirabilis*, l. 52. It may be worth observing that Reuben Brower, in a peculiarly "Horatian" study of the *Epistle to Bathurst*, failed to hear any echo of Horace in ll. 371–74; see his *Alexander Pope: The Poetry of Allusion* (Oxford: Clarendon, 1959), pp. 251–60 and passim.

[15] In connection with the myth of Danaë, the very expression that Professor Mack found so significant in Horace, viz., "converto in pretium deo," was used (in Greek) not only by Paulus Silentiarius but also by other poets of the *Greek Anthology*: Antipater (V.31.5) and Bassus (V.125.1). Cf. also Parmenion (V.33, 34), Asclepiades (V.64.6), Palladas (V.257.2), and Strabo (V.239.2).

[16] In his extensive notes to *Bathurst*, Pope draws our attention to echoes of Virgil (ll. 75, 184) and Juvenal (l. 394—copied by Johnson in *London*). If he had wished us to hear an echo of Horace in ll. 371–72, he could have provided a note as a pointer.

[17] I am using *decorate* in a favorable sense, as, for example, making a doctrine seductive. I am using *deepen* only in relation to meaning or doctrine.

Epistle to Bathurst) in such a way as to derive from them a coherent, convincing interpretation—unless that interpretation were so general as to depend on none of those allusions.

Similarly, I do not claim that I have found the correct sources of Pope's work, if there are sources—or that Professor Mack's learning has misled him. On the contrary, he may easily be right, and I may be wrong. I do claim that a reader learned enough to see an allusion to Horace's ode might at the same time recall any number of other associations with Pope's lines. If Pope was as alert as he seems to have been in the composition of this poem, he would not have presumed that even a classical scholar would make the connections Professor Mack has found.

General Allusions

General allusions, or allusions to context, offer a broader escape route from explicit meaning than one gains through isolated allusions. In these analyses the critic assumes that when a poet does echo a line or passage from a work by another poet, the reader ought to recall the whole of that earlier work and ought to use it as enlarging the significance of the poem at hand. The first question here is whether in any case there is such a general allusion. Scholars have a cheerful habit of assuming there is none when the earlier work would not fit their interpretative design. If Pope in *The Rape of the Lock* echoes MacSwiney's *Camilla*, most scholars are content to identify the borrowing and say no more. But if Pope echoes *Paradise Lost*, they bring to bear a whole system of Protestant theology in order to explicate the Roman Catholic's poem.

Earl Wasserman has suggested that in *The Rape of the Lock* when the heroine dreams of her guardian sylph Ariel, the poem invites us to think of *Paradise Lost* and of Satan tempting Eve.[18] If the poem does so, I should say it is by the subtlest of hints. But Ariel's speech certainly echoes the *Aeneid*, Psalm 91, and various poems by Dryden (as well as Milton's epic), as one may see from the notes to Tillotson's edition. It is also clear that the important echoes of *Paradise Lost* are from the speeches of the angels, Gabriel and Uriel, in Book IV—figures naturally associated with Ariel because they guard Eve as he guards Belinda. It is further clear that of all the echoes those of the *Aeneid* dominate the passage. If Professor Wasserman wished to make Ariel's character satanic, in opposition to all

[18] "The Limits of Allusion in *The Rape of the Lock*," *JEGP*, 65 (1966), 425–44. The late Professor Wasserman heard the parts of this essay dealing with his own scholarship when it was read before the English Institute.

these signs and to the sympathetic tone of the passage in Pope's poem, I cannot disprove his interpretation. But I can marvel at those who accept it.

I should like to call attention to one feature of Pope's work that may throw light on his allusiveness, although this feature is external to the poetry. In a few places Pope used a footnote to direct the reader's ear to a literary echo. It has been argued that the notes are a sign that Pope expected all such echoes, noted or not, to be observed.[19] But is this logical? Precisely the opposite seems to me the case. If Pope thought he could rely on the reader to recognize the echoes, he would supply no notes at all for the purpose. At one point he identifies a striking allusion to the opening line of the fourth book of the *Aeneid*. This was by far the best-known part of the best-known of all poems; and Pope felt he had to identify the allusion (*Rape of the Lock* IV.1). The existence of such notes suggests to me that the poet had a proper opinion of the illiteracy of his readers. Dryden's notes to *Annus Mirabilis* have equally cruel implications. And after all, even Montaigne had to read his adored Plutarch in French.

Since so many authors and works reecho through *The Rape of the Lock*, it becomes a subtle exercise to determine which of them, at many points, the poem may be following. But one should observe that at least three eighteenth-century critics—Dennis, Johnson, and Warton—considered the relation of the poem to its predecessors without observing any Virgilian or Miltonic parodies that Pope himself failed to annotate, and yet they discussed parallels with Boileau that Pope ignored. Dennis's *Remarks on the Rape of the Lock* are little more than a running comparison of Pope's masterpiece with Boileau's *Lutrin*. One might inquire whether the deficiency of these critics lay in their knowledge of Latin or of English.[20]

Even when a poet boldly alludes to another man's work and draws our attention to the fact, the significance of the parallel depends on how he applies it. We have no way of telling whether or not the poet asks us to recall the whole of the work he alludes to, we have no way of telling whether he supports or condemns the doctrine of that work, except from the use of the allusion in his own poem. Allusions are dumb witnesses until they are cross-examined.

For example, Professor Wasserman comments (pp. 433–34) on an echo

[19] Ibid., p. 425.

[20] See John Dennis, *Critical Works*, ed. E. N. Hooker (Baltimore: Johns Hopkins Press, 1939–43), II, 329, 341–42, and passim; Johnson, "Pope," par. 53–60, 335–41, in *Lives*, III, 101–4, 232–35; Joseph Warton, *An Essay on the Genius and Writings of Pope* (2 vols., 1756, 1782), passim; Alexander F. B. Clark, *Boileau and French Classical Criticism in England (1660–1830)* (Paris, 1925), p. 10 and passim.

of Psalm 91 in *The Rape of the Lock* and assumes that the poet intended it ironically, viz., that the satanic Ariel is ruining Belinda through the very language in which the Psalmist promises that God will protect the faithful (I.41–44). Professor Wasserman also comments on another couplet describing Belinda in words that recall Virgil's description of Dido when the queen burns with secret love for Aeneas. Here, Professor Wasserman says, there is a true parallel; and the poet, according to him, implies that Belinda, for all her coquetry, really desires to be loved just as Dido did.[21]

But supposing we admit that these two echoes are deliberate allusions to context; if we then wish to decide that one is ironical and the other straightforward, we must read Pope's poem. When we do so, I think it will appear that the first echo is used sympathetically and the second ironically. From the language and tone in which the poet explicitly and consistently describes the sylph, it is more probable that Ariel's character is benignly similar to that of Uriel and Gabriel than that it is devilishly opposed to theirs. In the words of the Psalmist, Ariel will defend Belinda against the dangers of night and day. As for the echo of Virgil's description of Dido, it is not through this that we discover Belinda's wish to be loved. On the contrary, it is through the explicit words of Pope in the preceding canto, which declare that an earthly lover lurks at her heart (*Rape* III.144). So there is nothing to be revealed in that department of her character. Describing Belinda as Dido, Pope says that "anxious cares the pensive nymph opprest, / And secret passions labour'd in her breast"; a few lines below, he explicitly enumerates the passions as "rage, resentment and despair," surely an ironical contrast to the amorous love consuming Dido (*Rape* IV.1–2, 9).

My attitude may be mistaken, and the art of *The Rape of the Lock* may indeed depend on the sort of reader who could treat all the parallels given in Tillotson's notes as general allusions. But whoever wishes to convert me to that view had better not start by declaring that Ariel is satanic, that Belinda is criminal, and that Clarissa, who hands the Baron the scissors when he wishes to cut the lock, is the character to whom we must look for moral enlightenment.[22] As for those who imagine that Pope systematically condemns Belinda's social environment for failing to meet the heroic standards of Achilles and Hector, they might do worse than to read Pope's translation of the *Iliad* and observe how deeply he

[21] Wasserman, p. 439; *Rape* IV.1; *Aeneid* IV.1. The identity of the line references in the *Rape* and the *Aeneid* is hardly accidental, and Pope's note would have been unnecessary if he had supposed he could trust the reader's memory of Virgil.

[22] I do not mean that Pope disagreed with Clarissa's advice but that he treated it here as a decorative formula.

was embarrassed by the coarseness, cruelty, boastfulness, and mendacity of Homer's heroes; and they might consider how much Pope perhaps thought Agamemnon could learn from the higher civilization of England under Queen Anne.

In the present essay my essential subject is not aspects of style but what might be called literary meanings, whether explicit or implicit. I attend to questions of style only as they involve the issue of explicitness. To many analyses of imagery, rhythm, and so forth, my complaints might be irrelevant. But the scholars whose work I examine claim to interpret the poems they handle, and they assume that their interpretations will convince rational, competent readers. It is in this framework that I point out their neglect of explicit meaning. In my view, literary meaning, explicit or implicit, is deliberate and appeals to a consensus. The great bulk of right readers are supposed to accept it.

But other kinds of meaning are of great interest and deserve careful attention. One is open meaning, the sort connected with modern literature. Here the reader is invited to supply his own associations and thus to complete the work, treating the text as an occasion for assembling meanings that no one else need share. Some of the interpretations I reject under the head of literary meaning might flourish under the head of open meaning. Thus Baudelaire's idiosyncratic interpretation of Poe is profoundly important. Yet another head will have to serve for the unconscious intentions of an author, those which the reader may attribute to him on the basis of a science of anthropology, psychology, or economics, but which do not seem deliberate aspects of the poem. Here also are meanings implicit in a myth or old story, which an unlearned adaptor may pass on without realizing that he does so. What is unconscious in one age becomes literary in another, especially as the criticism of earlier poetry inspires the writing of later poets. Freudian meanings in Shakespeare are unconscious; in O'Neill they are literary. For the esthetic critic of folklore, children's writing, or the art of primitive peoples, unconscious meanings are of essential value.

The world does not want for critics who dissolve the line between conscious and unconscious. In my view this dissolution sinks poetry to the level of grunts and growls. It is only through the habit of attributing deliberate intention to a speaker that we can handle unconscious meanings. The teller of an old story becomes no more than a phonograph or amanuensis when he passes on a tale that he himself does not understand. Through him we hear the original creator, whose meaning is purposeful. Unconscious meanings root themselves, for the interpreter, in an imitation of deliberate speech. The interpreter treats the unconscious aspect of the author as a separate creature with intentions of its own.

Parallel Poetry

The analysis of general allusions sometimes broadens to the point where works by two authors are set side by side as if the earlier were a consistently revealing parallel to the later. Here the scholar sometimes assumes that the model or source (if it is one) has fundamental meanings that are preserved (either sympathetically or ironically) in the later work. The result is what I call "parallel poetry." An age of mock-epics, mock-pastorals, and free translations seems peculiarly suited to this approach. If Fielding used the *Aeneid* as the general pattern for his novel *Amelia*, it seems fair to suspect that the role of Miss Matthews, who seduces the hero while they are both in the same jail, has moral implications like those which Virgil drew from Dido's seduction of Aeneas. But we can make the inference with confidence because Fielding explicitly passes on Captain Booth the same judgment that Mercury delivered to Aeneas.

When there is no explicit statement, our doubts cannot be easily resolved. A writer may use an earlier work as his pattern without adopting or rejecting its implications. Swift, in *The Battle of the Books*, based the action generally on that of the *Aeneid* and the *Iliad*. So he describes Wotton planning to kill Sir William Temple and echoes Virgil's description of Arruns planning to kill the female warrior Camilla. It is conceivable that some scholar might therefore identify Temple with Camilla and argue that Swift was making a comment on his patron's masculinity. Nobody could disprove such an argument and I dare not estimate how many would be persuaded by it.

Martin Price has tried to account for Dryden's *Absalom and Achitophel* largely in terms of *Paradise Lost*.[23] He frames this interpretation

[23] Price, *To the Palace of Wisdom* (New York: Doubleday, 1964), pp. 52–62. This line of interpretation goes back to A. W. Verrall, who called attention to Dryden's echoes of Milton and suggested that *Absalom and Achitophel* might be a miniature epic with satirical elements (*Lectures on Dryden*, ed. Margaret Verrall [Cambridge Univ. Press, 1914], pp. 55, 80, and passim). See also Van Doren, who said it was almost exclusively the diction of Milton—rather than anything else in his poetry—that influenced Dryden (end of chap. 3); E. M. W. Tillyard, *Poetry Direct and Oblique* (London: Chatto and Windus, 1934), pp. 81–88; Bonamy Dobrée, "Milton and Dryden: A Comparison in Poetic Ideas and Poetic Method," *ELH*, 3 (1936), 83–100; Ruth Wallerstein, "To Madness Near Allied: Shaftesbury and His Place in *Absalom and Achitophel*," *HLQ*, 6 (1943), 445–71 (and the perceptive review by H. Trowbridge, *PQ*, 23 [1944], 164); Ian Jack, *Augustan Satire: Intention and Idiom in English Poetry, 1660–1750* (Oxford: Clarendon, 1952), pp. 61–62 and n. 6 (replying acutely to Verrall); Morris Freedman, "Dryden's Miniature Epic," *JEGP*, 57 (1958), 211–19; Bernard Schilling, *Dryden and the Conservative Myth: A Reading of Absalom and Achitophel* (New Haven: Yale Univ. Press, 1961), pp. 136–37 and passim; Anne Davidson Ferry, *Milton and the Miltonic Dryden* (Cambridge, Mass.; Harvard Univ. Press, 1968), passim; Leonora Brodwin, "Miltonic Allusion in *Absalom and Achitophel*: Its Function in the Political Satire," *JEGP*, 58 (1969), 24–44.

in a scheme of moral principles derived from Pascal and Blake. So we are asked to understand the meaning of Dryden's poem not only in Milton's language but also in the categories of "energy," "order of the flesh," "order of the mind," and "order of the spirit." Now it happens that Dryden included in *Absalom and Achitophel* a long passage of sixty lines (752–810) clearly expounding the doctrine of his poem. This quite explicit passage Professor Price touches on in a few misleading sentences (p. 62), but to Dryden's supposed parallels with Milton he devotes paragraphs of analysis. His effort leads to surprising outcomes.

When Dryden calls the restive English people of 1681 "Adam-wits" (l. 51), Professor Price contrasts the term with Milton's view of Adam as a man of "intuitive wisdom" (p. 54). But Dryden is suggesting a parallel with Adam, not a contrast; and he does not allude to wisdom as such. The poet is saying that like Adam, many Englishmen do not appreciate true liberty when they possess it: in his words, they are "too fortunately free" (l. 51). Dryden's view was commonplace and anti-Puritan.[24] He is describing the Whigs here as rebellious Puritans, impatient of constitutional monarchy and demanding a republic. Later, in the passage of exposition, he makes the same point, in case the reader failed to grasp it earlier (ll. 755–56). Precisely the rebelliousness that Milton would approve, Dryden naturally condemned.

At one point Dryden uses the old simile of the human body in sickness for a political state in turmoil. The simile is made explicit both in the poem (ll. 136–41) and in the preface to the poem (ll. 61–64). Yet again Dryden produces it in the long expository passage (ll. 756, 809–10; cf. l. 926). Perhaps because Dryden describes feverish blood as a lake, Professor Price reads into the simile an improbable allusion to the geography of hell, which takes him back to *Paradise Lost* (p. 56).

Professor Price finds that Dryden relates Absalom's lawless self-indulgence to David's sexual promiscuity, and as a category to include both these impulses, Professor Price uses "energy." He then connects the unruliness of the people with the idea of energy and with sexual excess. But in fact Dryden explicitly attributes a rebellious nature to characters who are abstemious and who lack sexuality. In *Absalom and Achitophel* the poet never suggests that Absalom's depravity is related to his father's

[24] Cf. Strafford, writing in 1637 and arguing that men should trust the king "and rather attend upon his will, with confidence in his justice, belief in his wisdom, assurance in his parental affections to his subjects and kingdoms, than feed ourselves with curious questions, with the vain flatteries of imaginary liberty, which, had we even our silly wishes and conceits, were we to frame a new Commonwealth even to our own fancy, might in conclusion leave ourselves less free, less happy, than now, thanks be to God and his Majesty, we are" (C. V. Wedgwood, *Thomas Wentworth, First Earl of Strafford . . . A Revaluation* [London: Jonathan Cape, 1961], p. 239).

sexual habits, and the poem never links the unruliness of the people with either a general concept of energy or the king's promiscuity.

A Puritan might indeed do so; and in *Paradise Lost* Milton said that by letting their passions subdue their reason, men make themselves fit to be ruled by political tyrants—or kings (XI.90–101). But Dryden, as Professor Price observes, sets the free sexuality of King Charles against the abstinence of his enemy Lord Shaftesbury; for his lordship punishes "a body which he . . . could not please" (l. 167) and in place of many children begets one unpromising son. The poet associates Shaftesbury and his followers with Puritan "zeal" (l. 181) and with republican government (ll. 226–27). The poet says explicitly that the people's rebelliousness was innate (ll. 214–19) and not due to the king's character.

Anne Davidson Ferry has gone even further than Professor Price in founding an interpretation of *Absalom and Achitophel* upon Milton's work. Professor Ferry writes as though Dryden must have learned common biblical expressions like "sons of Belial" from *Paradise Lost*, even though the two poets give different implications to those words.[25] Scholars who follow this line of interpretation seldom remark that for both poets the Bible and the *Aeneid* were among the main sources of their greatest poem.[26] Some "Miltonic" scholars hardly admit that the story of David, Absalom, and Achitophel was repeatedly applied to kings in general and to Charles II in particular before Dryden wrote his satire.[27] They do not observe that the Satanism of Achitophel and the parallel with the Fall of Man were part of the tradition Dryden received. One sometimes gets the impression that when Moses wrote the Pentateuch, he was inspired less by Jehovah than by Milton.

[25] Ferry, p. 31; cf. James Kinsley's note on l. 598 of *Absalom and Achitophel* in his edition of Dryden's *Poems* (Oxford: Clarendon, 1958), IV, 1892.

[26] To most readers during the seventeenth century, the *Aeneid* would have seemed the normal model for large elements like the catalogue of heroes, the evil spirit from the underworld, and so on. For more particular references, see Reuben Brower, "Dryden's Epic Manner and Virgil," *PMLA*, 55 (Mar. 1940), 132–34; R. G. Peterson, "Larger Manners and Events: Sallust and Virgil in *Absalom and Achitophel*," *PMLA*, 82 (1967), 236–44. Even a line like Dryden's "He glides unfelt into their secret hearts" (l. 693), which might seem to echo Milton's "Into the heart of Eve his words made way" (IX.550), sounds more like Virgil's description of Allecto's serpent entering Amata (*Aeneid* VII.350–51); cf. Dryden's translation: "Unseen, *unfelt*, the fiery serpent *skims* . . . / His baleful breath inspiring as he *glides*. . . . / At first the silent venom slid with ease" (*Aeneid* VII.491–98, my italics).

[27] For anticipations of Dryden, see Hugh Macdonald, *John Dryden: A Bibliography of Early Editions and of Drydeniana* (Oxford: Clarendon, 1939), pp. 18–19; A. B. Chambers, "Absalom and Achitophel: Christ and Satan," *MLN*, 74 (1959), 592–96; Howard Schless, "Dryden's *Absalom and Achitophel* and *A Dialogue between Nathan and Absalome*," *PQ*, 40 (1961), 139–43; John M. Wallace, "Dryden and History: A Problem in Allegorical Reading," *ELH*, 36 (1969), 280–81; W. K. Thomas, "The Matrix of *Absalom and Achitophel*," *PQ*, 49 (1970), 92–99; Dryden, *Works*, ed. E. N. Hooker et al., II (Berkeley and Los Angeles: Univ. of California Press, 1972), 230–33.

Allusive interpretations are supposed to enrich a poem and add to its suggestiveness. But they can also impoverish, when they draw the reader away from brighter meanings. In one of Dryden's pictures of Absalom, Professor Ferry sees the features of Adam as shown in *Paradise Lost.* I quote Dryden's lines:

> His motions all accompanied with grace;
> And Paradise was open'd in his face.[28]
> [*Absalom and Achitophel,* ll. 29–30]

Others have heard Chaucer and Dante in these lines.[29] When I strain, I think I detect *Paradise Regain'd*, although I do not expect other men's ears to agree with my own.[30] But the issue is the effect of echo on meaning. Professor Ferry assumes that the poet treats Absalom as Adam. Yet the lines themselves explicitly state that grace goes with Absalom and that his face opens Paradise to the beholder. I see not a real Adam but a false messiah, particularly because elsewhere in the poem Absalom is explicitly named "Saviour" and "Messiah."[31] By fixing her eyes on a supposed source, Professor Ferry may have turned her back on a profound implication.

Parallels with *Paradise Lost* teach one little about the meaning of *Absalom and Achitophel.* Milton himself did not invent a story and give it meaning. Like Dryden he received a story that already carried familiar implications, those which a reader would know before he met *Paradise Lost.* In 1639 Strafford wrote about the attack of the Scots upon their rightful king and declared, "This is not a war of piety, for Christ's sake, but a war of liberty for their own unbridled, inordinate lusts and ambitions, such as threw Lucifer forth of Heaven."[32] Strafford was adapting a commonplace about Lucifer that both Milton and Dryden were to inherit.

Dryden at points may have described Achitophel in terms derived from Milton. But the great confrontation between Achitophel and Absalom recalls *Paradise Regain'd*, which Professor Price does not mention, more than *Paradise Lost.*[33] To press the parallels further than a similarity of action and rhetoric seems dangerous. It is one thing to regard Achitophel as satanic. Dryden in the poem explicitly describes him as false, cursed, secretive, crooked, ambitious, "implacable in hate." We don't

[28] See Ferry, p. 226, n. 5. Among the parallels she cited, I find only *Paradise Lost* VIII. 221–23 worth considering.

[29] See Kinsley's note on l. 30.

[30] Cf. *Paradise Regain'd* I.29–30, 67–68, 92–93, 280–81, 299–300. I do not believe these were intended by Dryden to be noticed by the reader of his poem.

[31] Ll. 230–40, 728. Cf. the article by Chambers.

[32] Cited by Wedgwood, p. 251.

[33] See Chambers.

need Milton to connect the devil with Achitophel.[34] But when Absalom is tempted by him, should we think of Eve? of Christ? of the fallen angels seduced by Lucifer? of all these? And if of all of these, does not the connotation become so general that it cannot matter if we omit any one of them?

Is it not a rash enterprise to hunt in a poem which attacks Puritan principles and exalts Charles II for the teachings of a poem which attacks monarchs as diabolical and exalts Puritan principles? If one had to set *Absalom and Achitophel* beside *Paradise Lost*, surely the correlation would be inverse. Where Dryden gave divine sanction to Charles II but identified the wicked Achitophel with democracy and rebellion, Milton described all kings as rebels against divine authority (XII.24–37) and linked Charles I to Satan (IV.393–94). One might perhaps read *Absalom and Achitophel* as a reply to *Paradise Lost*. It seems quixotic to read it as an echo.[35]

The action of Dryden's poem was indeed designed to recall that of another poem, but the other poem is neither *Paradise Lost* nor *Paradise Regain'd*. It is the Second Book of Samuel, chapters 13 to 19. Dryden made the Bible story the foundation of an allegorical history. Into this he may have incorporated large parallels with *Paradise Lost* and *Paradise Regain'd*; he certainly alluded to the rest of the Second Book of Samuel and to other books of the Bible, not to mention the *Aeneid* and Ovid's *Metamorphoses*. To single out *Paradise Lost* from this complex and to make it the unique highway into Dryden's argument seems a flight from explicit meaning.

Moral Traditions

The broadest and most evocative parallel with another literary work is still less liberating than the removal of a poem from one great moral tradition to another. When a scholar sets aside the explicit elements and employs allusions, imagery, and figures of speech so as to reclassify a poem in an order of doctrines it has never been pictured with, one sees shutters opening and one gasps at vistas of forbidden landscapes. Generally, a scholar uses this route in order to arrive at a subversive meaning for a poem that had seemed orthodox. But the purpose may also be to reduce

[34] "References to Shaftesbury as a rebellious *diabolus* are common"—Kinsley, note to ll. 52–53. Dryden in the dedication of *All for Love* (1678) said those who claimed England would be better off with a change of government were following Satan, their ancestor, who tried to seduce mankind into following him in his own rebellion.

[35] Brodwin has interpreted *Absalom and Achitophel* as a tissue of ironical allusions to Milton's works. According to her, the poem requires the reader not only to recognize the allusions but to understand that they are generally unsympathetic to Milton.

an apparently iconoclastic poem to orthodox morality. When the explicit elements clash with the new interpretation, we have the interesting case of a work that seems openly daring but that is—or so the critic says—insidiously conventional.

I must again make some distinctions. In examining the meaning of a poem, one finds some opinions or generalizations that seem particularly to be enforced by the argument, structure, and connotations. These I call the doctrine. There are others that appear as commonplaces with which nobody could disagree. They are taken for granted as casual opinion, neither recommended nor attacked. These I call formulae.

The more commonplace a principle is, the more emphatic an author has to be if he wishes to make a point of teaching it—or presenting it as doctrine rather than assuming it as formula. A contempt for the mob of common people, an admiration for the English political constitution, when casually expressed, cannot be significant. It must be a formula. If a writer takes a principle for granted in his work, the alert reader will assume little from it about the meaning of the work. This is particularly so in the period 1660–1760, when doctrines that are not scandalous, blasphemous, or politically subversive are normally expounded as well as illustrated. In a dramatic work this is supremely true, because unless the doctrine is explicitly conveyed by a sympathetic character, we have no way of telling whether it is a commonplace formula, a peculiar trait of one of the characters, or a genuine doctrine advocated by the author.

Now no religious principle is more commonplace, more widely accepted—by ancient Greeks, by Mohammedans, and by Christians—than that of divine Providence, the principle that the gods intervene in human life so as to assist the virtuous and frustrate the wicked. In the finest comedies of the Restoration period few readers have found this doctrine expounded or illustrated, because the explicitly amoral character of the protagonists is so striking. From Dorimant in *The Man of Mode* to Mirabell in *The Way of the World* the man on whom fortune smiles lacks the marks of Christian goodness.

Aubrey Williams has recently decided that this view is wrong, and he has argued that in fact the plays of Congreve are "brilliant demonstrations of a providential order in human event that is fully analogous to the greater world of providential order insisted upon not only by contemporary Anglican theologians but also insisted upon by contemporary literary critics as a fundamental dramatic principle. . . . the works of Congreve are fully conformable to the Christian vision of human experience which still prevailed at the end of the seventeenth century."[36] Professor

[36] "Poetical Justice, the Contrivances of Providence, and the Works of William Congreve," *ELH*, 35 (1968), p. 541.

Williams supported this lively departure from received opinion by analyzing the structure and the language of the plays. He tried to show that Congreve dramatized the Christian idea through complicated plots which fit the descriptions given by literary critics and by priests of the workings of providential justice. Instead of surveying all his analyses of Congreve's works, I shall examine the pair that seem crucial.

I myself would think twice before identifying as a Christian principle the belief that God intervenes on the side of virtue. As a religious institution Christianity has never lacked presumption. But we need not add to the wealth of so prosperous a corporation this commonest of properties. Elaborate plots in which the schemes of villains are defeated by sympathetic characters through the operation of surprising coincidences are the mainstay of comedy from Menander to Molière. It would be a delicate job of carpentry to join the use of such plots to any one moral philosophy or religious doctrine. *Love for Love* is a play that gives much attention to supernatural interventions in human affairs. One reason is that a butt in the play is an amateur astrologer named Foresight. Professor Williams says *Love for Love* is "saturated with Christian imagery and diction," and that there is no evidence for calling its perspective "naturalistic" (p. 559). But he spreads out the net of Christian language till it catches the many references to prophecies that are or are not fulfilled in connection with Foresight's obsession; he includes religious expressions that are part of common speech; and he treats figurative language as literal. Would it be unkind to observe that in this sense *The Land of Heart's Desire* and *Sunday Morning* are saturated with Christian imagery and diction? Nowhere in *Love for Love* is the doctrine of a providential order explicitly discussed. The references to it (if they are such) remain casual and formulaic.

Yet *Love for Love* does exhibit a remarkable density of religious terms or allusions. The heroine is named Angelica; the hero is Valentine. The hero's father, Sir Sampson Legend, is explicitly connected with his biblical namesake; and the surname Legend might possibly be a play on the word *scripture*. Foresight's name is simply English for providence. The comedy opens with a burlesque discussion of stoic apathy, which quickly seems contrasted with a kind of love that might be called Christian. In the first hundred and fifty lines of the play we meet figures of speech referring to canonization, doomsday, the devil, and martyrdom. Two ladies of weak virtue in the play visit a pleasure palace called The World's End. In one scene a rake teaches a silly girl a catechism of love (II.i.598–661). In another scene, Valentine, pretending to be mad, echoes the words of Christ and babbles about religious doctrines (IV.i.251–59, 486–514). At the end of the play the religious allusions grow as dense as they are at the start. In one bit of repartee Valentine draws explicit parallels between true love and Christian salvation. Another character compares Angelica's conduct to divine justice and the conversion of infidels. In the curtain speech, Angelica herself compares true love to true faith, martyrdom, and miracles. Finally, the design of the epilogue depends on the ideas of Providence, transmigration of souls, salvation, and damnation.

How are we to treat this crowd of allusions? To begin with, we may set aside the possibility of accident. So strong a concentration was surely deliberate. Therefore we face several choices. The pattern may add up to an allusive argument for the existence of Providence. It may be an ironic but serious reference to high religious principles by which the amoral trivialities of the play are found wanting. Or it may constitute a comic parallel between sexual passion and religious devotion, following the old tradition which suggests that for lovers the trifling details of courtship are as important as salvation; poems by Donne and Marvell provide some celebrated examples of the tradition. What we must not claim (although Professor Williams has nearly done so) is that the mere presence of such material reveals an author's views on religion. Ben Jonson's and Swift's concentrated parodies of Puritan language may have more to do with Congreve's plays than the sermons of Anglican divines.

Harriett Hawkins has shown how the sides are drawn.[37] Collier, Congreve, and Samuel Johnson ("Congreve," in *Lives*, III, 222) are among those who found the pattern either comic or blasphemous. Professor Williams and other scholars have argued against them and treat the pattern as having serious, positive implications (Hawkins, pp. 101–5). Readers of taste, learning, and great intelligence have thus come to contrary judgments. As Professor Hawkins observes, such variety alone indicates that the tone of the allusions cannot be determined by isolating them from the play as a whole. She also reminds us that religious images are staples of Restoration comic dialogue and erotic verse. Consequently, if a playwright employed them for amoral, witty effects, he was in no way eccentric (Hawkins, pp. 103–7).

So we learn that like all other allusions, those to religious traditions have no necessary implications. They too are silent witnesses. If I invoke my distinction between formulae and doctrines, I find that while the doctrines touched on in *Love for Love* are utterly commonplace, the allusions to them are casual, brief, and disconnected; there is nothing in this play like the explicit discussions of the doctrine of Providence in Johnson's *Irene*. Again, therefore, I must class the effect as formulaic.

To determine the tone or meaning, we are left with nothing but context. Yet the force of the context here is surely decisive. The author of

[37] *Likenesses of Truth in Elizabethan and Restoration Drama* (Oxford: Clarendon, 1972), pp. 98–108.

Love for Love must have been an inexperienced blunderer if he intended us to take seriously his references to religion. For he juxtaposes and mingles them with so much bawdy, coarse, or blasphemous conversation —all with no hint of blame—that a serious attitude is not conceivable. Only by abstracting the religious allusions from the play and studying them as independent matter can one even spasmodically suppose the playwright intended them to support Christian morals. The point of the religious imagery and language is surely comic and parodical, to suggest that sexual passion is a lover's religion. Maximillian Novak has shrewdly connected the plot of *Love for Love* with Boccaccio's tale of Federigo, who pauperizes himself trying (and failing) to seduce the virtuous young matron Giovanna and is crowned at last with her hand and fortune after her husband dies (*Decameron*, V.9).[38] I think some such idea of enthusiastic martyrdom for carnal love underlies the game Congreve was playing.

To describe sexual passion in the language of religious devotion is an old, charming habit of poets from Ovid onwards, although pious judges have found it blasphemous. Congreve could hardly appear freakish if he made characters in *Love for Love* adopt this practice. When Valentine (who regrets that the baby farmer looking after one of his bastards has not smothered it) finally secures the heroine to be his bride, he says to one of his rivals, "You would have interposed between me and Heav'n; but Providence laid Purgatory [i.e., marriage by trickery, to a promiscuous woman] in your way—You have but Justice" (V.i.595–97). Professor Williams takes this remark as an indication of Congreve's theology and asks, "How much more explicit can a playwright possibly be about the Providential relevance of the poetical justice he has exemplified in a play?" (p. 560). One hesitates to reply, the choice is so varied. Surely Congreve did not believe in the doctrine of purgatory!

To describe Valentine, the hero of *Love for Love*, as "exemplifying the traditional Christian paradox that one kind of madness occasionally to be found in this world may be, in the eyes of Heaven, the highest kind of wisdom"—as Professor Williams also does (pp. 559–60)—demonstrates the happy elasticity of the word *Christian*. Valentine, who has wasted his fortune in pleasure for the sake of Angelica, pretends insanity to avoid being disinherited and to make Angelica confess that she loves him. When his scheme fails and he believes Angelica will marry his own father, he agrees in despair to give up his claim to the estate. She is then so deeply touched by his fidelity that she finally declares her love. Professor Williams contrasts Valentine with the other characters, who "seek their own most selfish purposes" while the hero "is willing to be mad

38 *William Congreve* (New York: Twayne, 1971), p. 108; cf. p. 89, on "religious imagery . . . put to the service of a libertine ethic."

enough to ruin himself for love of another" (pp. 559–60). But alas the selfishness of the other characters—such as it is—consists largely in their wishing to enjoy the sexual pleasures that Valentine has been enjoying and to marry a fortune as Valentine wishes to do. In the matter of deceit it would take an expert casuist to settle the precedence between Valentine and his rivals. Professor Williams found Congreve's plays providential in design because he concentrated on the character of the villains. Those who examine the heroes will find them pagan.

As Professor Williams observes, Congreve made no explicit reference to Providence as such in *The Way of the World*. Yet Professor Williams discerns in the magnificent complexity of the plot and the happy resolution of Marwood's devilish schemes Congreve's "most polished justification of the contrivances of Providence" (p. 562). To illustrate what he means, he quotes from the *Essay on Man* (II.175). To which I reply, Just so: Pope explicitly argued in support of the doctrine, and because it was so commonplace, he argued with great emphasis and clarity. Congreve did not.

It is confusing to hear a scholar declare that some works must teach Christian providential doctrine because they explicitly argue for it, while other works must do so because they exemplify it with no overt declaration. In fact, however, even if an epilogue appeared at the end of *The Way of the World* to say that the play was a demonstration of divine Providence, I would dismiss the declaration as a formula. In the character of Mirabell what is there to deserve divine intervention? The fact that when he thought his castoff mistress was pregnant, he married her to an old friend? Just how does Mirabell display faith, hope, and charity? It is surely because the evil of characters like Marwood is matched by no saintly goodness on the other side that the plays cannot embody any transcendental moral doctrine. If we transfer Restoration comedies from the theater to the classroom, we may give them sober weight by reading into them doctrines respected (though not held) by our own students. But if we remain true to the language and action of the plays, we must reject the opportunity.

Allegory

Critics who slur over the explicit parts of a poem often seem to rely on a shaky postulate. This is the view that all the elements of a poem should cohere, that no part may lack great significance, that no digression may serve as mere decorative entertainment. Each monad then must have meaning in its own right, and its meaning must possess an important relation to that of all the others. Every striking effect of versification must be parallel to a striking sense. Every subplot must somehow reflect the main plot. The design of the action cannot be pleasingly symmetrical; its symmetry must suggest a divine symmetry, or else it must be ironically contrasted to social chaos. I think this kind of totalitarian analysis debases the idea of organic form, which properly refers to a harmony of conception that liberates the means of expression.

When the critic tries to apply false notions of coherence to a poem, he sometimes finds no allusions or parallels that will integrate a stubborn passage into his scheme. If he cannot let the passage stand as diverting ornament, or as one of many possible developments of the original conception, if he must pry a suitable meaning out of it and stamp it firmly into a design, he may at last choose the literary equivalent of *mettre à la question*, that is, an interpretation through allegory. Now it is unlikely that an Augustan poet would erect an allegory in a poem without warning the reader—unless the meaning were blasphemous, immoral, or subversive. For Augustans, allegory was not a device for concealing a secret doctrine; it was an entertaining way of representing truths. Whoever reviews those works with allegorical elements, from Butler's *Hudibras* to Johnson's Oriental tales, will find them overequipped with explication. One thinks of the debates in *Pilgrim's Progress*, the expository passages of *Absalom and Achitophel*, the notes to the *Dunciad*, the rehearsal framework of Fielding's *Historical Register*. When Dryden wrote *The Hind and the Panther*, he rendered the genre and the argument of his poem perhaps too clear. In Fielding's farce the poet says, "Sir, this scene is writ in allegory; and though I have endeavoured to make it as plain as possible, yet all allegory will require a strict attention to be understood, sir" (II.i). The reference to strict attention is sarcastic; only a deaf mute could miss the point of the scene that follows.

But Brendan O Hehir has taken another approach to Denham's overpraised piece of topographical verse, *Cooper's Hill*.[39] This is a long poem which deals with a series of prospects to be seen from a hill near Windsor and with the associations—historical and political—of those prospects. As Denham in the poem thinks of various moral and political doctrines, he discusses them explicitly until two-thirds of the way through, when he describes a stag hunt that occupies most of the remainder (ll. 241–322, out of 358 lines in the entire poem). Now the hunt could easily have suggested to his readers several Aesopian fables in which a stag figures;[40] and in one couplet the fleeing stag is compared explicitly with a statesman in disgrace (ll. 273–74). But in the bulk of the poem Denham explicitly

[39] *Expans'd Hieroglyphics: A Study of Sir John Denham's* Cooper's Hill *with a Critical Edition of the Poem* (Berkeley and Los Angeles: Univ. of California Press, 1969).

[40] Cf. the three in John Ogilby's *Fables*, 2nd ed. (1668), nos. 28 (p. 67), 37 (p. 88), 45 (p. 109).

produces any doctrines that the prospects evoke for him; so one would not expect him suddenly to turn utterly emblematic.

Professor O Hehir cannot believe the stag is so loosely connected with the political and historical argument he finds in the poem. He therefore interprets the hunt as allegory and discovers it to represent the fall of King Charles I. Unhappily for this imaginative design, the royalist poet explicitly describes the hunt as innocent and happy. The poet also describes Charles I as leading the hunt; and finally he describes Charles as killing the stag.

I shall not go into the details of Professor O Hehir's argument. He saw at once the obstacles I have pointed out, and he ingeniously, if not wisely, disposed of them. What he did not dispose of is this question. If the poet intended the deer to represent the king, why did he explicitly say the king hunted and killed the deer? Or if he was giving an allegorical account of the supreme historical tragedy of his lifetime, why did he explicitly associate it with such epithets as "innocent" and "happy"? Why did the poet through his explicit remarks throw the reader off the track of the emblematic meaning? What did he gain? It is hardly conceivable that a poet should deliver his account of an event familiar to every possible reader in a form that would mislead all but the most curious and subtle.

If a scholar chooses to find Professor O Hehir's meanings in *Cooper's Hill*, the force impelling him must surely be the desire to deepen and enrich a poem of which Dr. Johnson accurately said, "The digressions are too long, the morality too frequent, and the sentiments sometimes such as will not bear a rigorous enquiry" (life of Denham, par. 29). The way the scholar deepens and enriches it would seem, I think, to endow it with the power that Symbolist and post-Symbolist poets attributed to their images. Professor O Hehir tried to make the poem suggestive and emblematic in the way that Ezra Pound once hoped his ideograms would be. But in doing so, he defied and flew from the explicit language of the poet.[41] One wonders whether Professor O Hehir thought an obscure allegory would please critics better than a decorative hunting scene. Scholars often assume that any literary device—irony, allegory, allusion—is

[41] Earl Wasserman, in a study to which Professor O Hehir is mightily indebted, first gave the stag hunt an allegorical interpretation; but he decided it represented the trial and death of Lord Strafford (*The Subtler Language*, [Baltimore: Johns Hopkins Press, 1959], pp. 72–76). Ruth Nevo, in *The Dial of Virtue: A Study of Poems on Affairs of State in the Seventeenth Century* (Princeton Univ. Press, 1963), accepted Professor Wasserman's interpretation; but Professor O Hehir has disproved it. Speaking frivolously, I should say that if the stag hunt must be interpreted as an allegory of the life of a king, the subject is more likely Richard II than Charles I: Richard's badge was a white hart, and he was indeed destroyed by a king. There is also an epigram by Martial (I.xxx) on a mock-chase in the amphitheater, during which a hind, flying from hounds, stopped as a suppliant before the emperor.

more admirable than no literary device. They conveniently forget that a poet cannot accept the gifts on his right hand without surrendering those on his left. If the stag hunt is allegorical, the poet was inept. If it is not allegorical, the poem lacks coherence. In either case, the scholar has failed to enhance the merit of the work.

Professor O Hehir avoided committing himself unqualifiedly to the interpretation I have summarized. If his argument is bold, his hedges are visible. But Professor Wasserman, in a similar use of allegory, refuses to allow for other interpretations than his own, which he insists is correct in every detail.[42] The passage I have in mind is fifty-odd lines from Pope's *Windsor Forest*. These lines deal with the nymph Lodona, who belonged to Diana when the goddess lived in Windsor Forest. One day, Pope says, Lodona wandered outside the forest and was seen by Pan, who loved her at once and wished to rape her. Lodona ran to preserve her chastity. But Pan was too fast. So Diana saved the nymph by turning her into the river Loddon.

Professor Wasserman declares that Windsor Forest represents England in a state of harmony, that Lodona represents the English people straying from harmony into the War of the Spanish Succession, and that Pan represents war. Pope himself nowhere says any of this, and he neither echoes nor alludes to another poem that does so. Professor Wasserman's allegory depends first on the description Pope gave of the nymph; next, on her "straying" outside the forest during a hunt; and finally, on the character of Pan.

Pope describes Lodona as looking very much like Diana and as scorning both the praise and the care of beauty. Lodona loves hunting; she wears a simple belt around her waist, a fillet around her hair, a quiver on her shoulder. Professor Wasserman declares that in her indifference to her own beauty the nymph reveals a contempt for the principle of order. Since Pope nowhere says this, it must be inferred. Yet the explicit language of the passage seems praise of Lodona:

> Scarce could the goddess from her nymph be known,
> But by the crescent and the golden zone,
> She scorn'd the praise of beauty, and the care;
> A belt her waste, a fillet binds her hair,
> A painted quiver on her shoulder sounds,
> And with her dart the flying deer she wounds.
>
> [ll. 175–80]

The nymph is as chaste and beautiful as Diana, but (in keeping—dare I say so?—with a well-known *topos*) hunting means more to her than sexual passion, and she is not vain. This sounds to me like explicit praise.

[42] *Subtler Language*, pp. 133–39.

And what are the literary sources of Pope's description, if one seeks possible echoes? The chief sources turn out to be Dryden's descriptions of Venus and Camilla in his translation of the *Aeneid*—hardly censorious allusions, as any reader of them will learn.

Pope says that in her eagerness to hunt the deer, Lodona wandered out of the forest—"Beyond the forest's verdant limits stray'd" (l. 182). Professor Wasserman says this act suggests a movement out of the realm of order and nature's law, into chaos (p. 137), a movement which in turn suggests the involvement of the English people in the War of the Spanish Succession. Pope mentions neither order nor law nor war nor chaos. So the meaning must be inferred. Now if one leaves the forest, where does one go? Pope explicitly says that beside the forest, in his landscape, are pasture and tillage (l. 37), fruitful fields (l. 26), Ceres' gifts (l. 39), yellow harvests (l. 88). Are we to suppose the poem, by a movement out of a forest into cultivated fields, represents a descent from order into chaos? Why should a poet choose a nymph explicitly associated with cold water and chastity to represent a nation plunging into war?

Professor Wasserman, in his account, repeats the word "stray'd" as if Pope employed it pejoratively. But earlier in *Windsor Forest* the poet applied the word to the motion of Diana herself (l. 165), and in his translation of the *Aeneid* Dryden gives us the original of Pope's expression when Venus appears dressed as a huntress and asks Aeneas and Achates whether they have seen a sister huntress who "in the forest stray'd" (I.445). The word means no more than "wandered" or "roamed."

Pope says Pan saw Lodona, loved her, and "burning with desire" pursued her. Professor Wasserman says Pan can be identified with disorder and chaotic war (p. 137). Pope says nothing of the sort, only that Pan saw, loved, and pursued the nymph. So any further meaning must be inferred. For his own inference Professor Wasserman turned to Francis Bacon's *De Sapientia Veterum*, but this is not a book which Pope is known to have read. If one searches *Windsor Forest* itself, one meets Pan as the familiar god of shepherds and pastures in the famous line, "See Pan with flocks, with fruits Pomona crown'd" (l. 37). And if one examines Pope's *Pastorals*, composed at the same time as the bulk of *Windsor Forest*, one meets Pan yet again as a pastoral god (*Autumn*, l. 81). It is possible that a poet would employ the god of shepherds, in contrast to the goddess of hunters, as the emblem of war; but few critics would praise him for doing so.

If the poem does embody an allegory so much at odds with its explicit meaning, we have the right to ask why the poet should have felt so indifferent to the clear sense of his words. The argument of *Windsor Forest* is neither immoral nor blasphemous nor dangerous to the government in power. Why then did Pope wish to mislead his reader?

I suggest that this allegory may be another flight from explicit meaning and that the scholar who invented it may have longed to disclose in Pope a kind of organic form and symbolic evocativeness that is, rightly or wrongly, more often observed in the poetry of the last hundred and eighty years.[43] In the elucidation of Augustan literature I wonder whether any obstacle is so great as the nineteenth century, which operates like a young surgeon lifting the face of his mother.

Irony

Allegorical interpretations, whether or not they seem probable, must start from the creatures and actions represented in a literary work. The critic may give the persons and their deeds a symbolic meaning, but he is still limited by the materials he finds. He must carry a supply of learning to his task. There is another method of flying from the explicit meaning of a work without facing these barriers. That is to give the work an ironical interpretation. For the Augustan writer, indirect methods of conveying a moral principle—especially irony and impersonation—were important. The demand for an appearance of rational clarity often prevented the Augustan from offering his reader more colorful means of participating in the work of creation. But the reader can feel agreeably that he is inventing, discovering, or at least uttering the doctrine if he must evolve it himself in a pleasant or playful unmasking.

During the middle third of the twentieth century irony received a eulogistic implication which few critics would now take exception to. This implication probably grew out of the effort to recommend both the poetry and the taste of men like Eliot and Pound to an academic audience. The work of the Metaphysicals and that of the modernists troubled those readers who identified the lyric with the poems of Keats and Shelley. In order to alter taste, critics altered the language of taste; and irony, which had seemed opposed to poetry, soon coalesced with it.

At first it was the rhetorical device of irony that critics commended, i.e., pretending ignorance when one is wise, or saying the opposite of what one means, or praising through blame and blaming through praise. But Richards, Empson, and Cleanth Brooks broadened the concept, and irony came to mean the inclusion of alternatives in a poet's proffering of any moral position. (This is somehow regarded as always praiseworthy.) Soon Kierkegaardian irony joined the others, and Existentialist praise of a fundamentally ambiguous moral attitude further enriched the concept. At the same time, by a parallel movement in the analysis of the Jamesian and Conradian novel, the idea of an unreliable narrator became more

[43] Professor Wasserman had a very different view of what he was doing; see ibid., pp. 3–12.

and more fashionable until an author who clearly knew what was happening in his story and obviously regarded some characters as worse than others began to seem fatally incompetent. The ironic approach to all genres now appears a most efficient method of redeeming poems or stories that seem sunk in dullness or inconsistency, for it lands them on a shore where ambiguity, uncertainty, and amorality are the signs of grace. This approach is an old one in classical studies, where a great scholar has called it the "last expedient of a despairing commentator."[44]

The main device of critics so inclined is to show that the narrator or speaker of a story or poem is not only distinct from the author but an object of the author's contempt. The critic assumes that the author deliberately chose, for greater artfulness, not to reveal his attitude openly. So the explicit meaning of the work is treated a priori as only apparently explicit. What the author seems to praise, he blames; where he seems sympathetic, he is really contemptuous.

How are we to know this? The critic postulates that the author is a well-known genius; his work is accepted as a remarkable achievement. Therefore, if its apparent faults and inconsistencies can dissolve themselves in an ironical interpretation, that ought to be preferred to a simple interpretation. Where the genius appears to be blundering (says the critic), especially where he seems to recommend a moral judgment that no genius should hold, we are justified in looking for irony.

For example, Robert Hopkins has decided that in Goldsmith's *Vicar of Wakefield* the protagonist and narrator, Dr. Primrose, is "an object of satire who is both a clergyman and a fortune-hunter, as well as a professor of optimistic platitudes. His complacency is nauseous, and there is a smugness about the Vicar, who is writing his own romance with himself as the hero, who has seen his platitudes vindicated by experience, and who is in effect telling us that he was right all along."[45] Professor Hopkins says that if we take this view of the novel, it will be a better work than if we do not.

I have two preliminary comments to make. First, it is not self-evident that if your interpretation makes a literary work sound better than it did before, the interpretation is validated. Second, the judgment that a work is ironical in mode does not automatically make the work better than a simpler view would make it.

Like the bulk of critics who wish to transform a simple narrator into an object of the author's contempt, Professor Hopkins gives most of his attention to the proof that the Vicar is such an object. He rarely stops to consider whether the novel as a whole would gain if we agree with him. For example, Professor Hopkins finds that the Vicar confuses, in his

44 Eduard Fraenkel, *Horace* (Oxford: Clarendon, 1957), p. 46, n. 2.

45 *The True Genius of Oliver Goldsmith* (Baltimore: Johns Hopkins Press, 1969), p. 208.

speech, the terms of commerce and the language of religion—as when the Vicar calls his beloved children "treasures" (pp. 211–12). Now if we agreed that Goldsmith was indeed exposing the narrator's materialism and hypocrisy by putting such metaphors into his mouth, would we not also have to blame Goldsmith for treating the language of Christ, St. Paul, St. Augustine, and generations of saints as hypocritical? There is nothing in Dr. Primrose's language that is not a commonplace of Christian homiletics. The more ironical Goldsmith's intention was, therefore, the greater his deafness to verbal associations must have been, and the more ignorantly he must have misled his readers.

Another piece of evidence, according to Professor Hopkins, is the clichés into which Goldsmith's style sinks when he represents a particularly sentimental or absurd action. One must agree with Professor Hopkins that the style in these scenes is indeed ridden with clichés of sentiment and expression. The difficulty is that it is so elsewhere as well. If the texture of language shifted radically at the points Professor Hopkins exhibits, Goldsmith would have been the kind of artist Professor Hopkins generously desires him to be. Unfortunately, it does not. If, therefore, those scenes were intended to be ironical, how are we to be sure the others were not as well? If they were, the structure of the novel becomes chaotic enough to satisfy Robbe-Grillet himself.

Professor Hopkins believes that the author is condemning the narrator out of his own mouth when the Vicar delivers prudential maxims that ill consort with the character of a Christian priest—who, according to Professor Hopkins, ought to be a martyr to rigorist benevolism. This may be so, and I wish it were. But if it is so, what are we to do with all the other characters in the book, saintly and satanic, who deliver the same maxims? Are we to assume that they too were being riddled with irony?

There is also the problem of the ending. Suppose the reader is expected to respond with contempt to the character of the hypocritical, avaricious Vicar? Why then did Goldsmith make him as happy as possible at the end of the novel? Is this the subtlest stroke of his irony? Or are we to agree with Professor Hopkins that the "happy ending does not diminish the satire on optimism" (p. 225)? If it does not, the novelist was amazingly indifferent to the language his readers knew. "I had nothing now on this side of the grave to wish for," says the Vicar at the end; "all my cares were over; my pleasure was unspeakable." If this is the way Goldsmith treated the character we are to reject, he may have been a profound ironist, but his skill as a novelist must lie in doubt.

Professor Hopkins was able to give his analysis a thin topping of plausibility only by treating the Vicar in isolation from the rest of the persons in the story. Who can doubt that the Vicar is imperfect? He is too trusting, and fails (like Abraham Adams and Squire Allworthy) to see through deceit and hypocrisy. He sometimes commits moral errors for which he reproaches himself (as at the close of chap. 13). He is not strong enough in maintaining his own standards against the willfulness of his wife and daughters. Besides, although the Vicar is telling his story in the first person, he is sometimes ironical at his own expense and is sometimes made an object of humorous dramatic irony by Goldsmith. Above all, the plot of the story and the finest dramatic ironies depend on his concealing from us his knowledge of two facts: that Mr. Burchell (who admires his younger daughter Sophia and seems to be a drifting, penniless man of feeling) is really the rich, philanthopic Sir William Thornhill, and that Mr. Thornhill, Sir William's young nephew and the Vicar's landlord (and who also admires Sophia), is a complete villain. In telling his story, the Vicar dwells on the errors that his ignorance led him into; and it is these that produce both the dramatic ironies and the exposure of his weaknesses. But if we observe the covetous man to whom Goldsmith systematically opposed him in the novel—that is, Mr. Wilmot—we learn that while prudence is in everyone's mouth, there is a difference between the greed that would sacrifice moral principles to material gain and the virtue that takes a rational view of what is required by sublunary bodies.

It seems to me that in all flights from explicit meaning the modern critic subscribes to the common view that statement is never preferable to suggestion in poetry. René Wellek and Austin Warren have said, "We reject as poetry or label as mere rhetoric everything which persuades us to a definite outward action. Genuine poetry affects us more subtly. Art imposes some kind of framework which takes the statement of the work out of the world of reality."[46] In literature written before the Romantic movement this declaration would have been unthinkable. The elements of style and structure were then conceived as decorating, enhancing, giving life to an argument or narrative; and tragedy, epic, history, oratory were central genres. When the lyric genres triumphed, the value of implication soared; and the explicit meaning became a disposable topsoil out of which grew the flowers of metaphor, irony, dramatic speech, allegory, allusion. Today without even recognizing their presupposition, too many critics believe that when they have found irony, allusiveness, or dramatic speech in a poem, they have established its literary excellence.

One of the most startling invocations of the concept of the ironical speaker is an analysis recently applied to Swift's best-known poem. The last third of *Verses on the Death of Dr. Swift* reads like a eulogy of the author put in the mouth of a speaker who is supposed to be an impartial acquaintance. The result, which amounts to self-praise, is gross at points and generally disgusts the literary palate. Barry Slepian has tried to show that the contradiction between the claims made for Swift in these lines

[46] *Theory of Literature* (New York, 1956), chap. 2, p. 13.

and the reality of his writings and public deeds is so violent that the claims must be ironical, and that Swift here must be mocking himself as a final case of the vanity condemned earlier in the poem.[47] We are faced, then, with two alternatives: either Swift blows his own horn, or he sends himself up.[48]

One may state it as a general proposition that when a critic tries to impose an ironical interpretation upon a straightforward passage, he must work against a formidable and coherent body of circumstantial evidence: the context of the passage, the normal marks of the author's work, the demands of genre, and various historical and biographical facts. Like other critics employing his approach, Dr. Slepian has abstracted from the poem and its circumstances a few elements that seem incompatible. Like the other critics, he then describes the poet as so careful an artist that he could not have ignored such irregularities. And like the other critics, he also assumes that if the passage is ironical, it will be better poetry than if it is straightforward.

I don't know how one can prove that any remark, including the present sentence, is not ironical. But I can suggest that an ironical interpretation creates greater irregularities than it removes. To begin externally, the poem was published with notes by Swift that sound perfectly straightforward and that require a serious interpretation of the lines quoted by Dr. Slepian. Features that some critics treat as ironical in the poem itself reappear with no trace of irony in the notes. These notes are repetitious, vindictive, and cranky. They explicitly puff Swift and his friends. They explicitly damn his enemies. Often they are false.

Dr. Slepian declares (p. 254) that some lines in the text of the poem are false, e.g., line 460: "He lash'd the vice but spar'd the name."[49] Here Dr.

47 "The Ironic Intention of Swift's Verses on His Own Death," *RES*, n. s. 14 (1963), 249–56. For responses to Dr. Slepian's arguments see Edward Rosenheim, review of the article, in *PQ*, 43 (1964), 392; Marshall Waingrow, "*Verses on the Death of Dr. Swift*," *SEL*, 5 (1965), 513–18; Ronald Paulson, *The Fictions of Satire* (Baltimore: Johns Hopkins Press, 1967), pp. 189–91; John Irwin Fischer, "How to Die: *Verses on the Death of Dr. Swift*," *RES*, n. s. 21 (1970), 422–41; Arthur H. Scouten and Robert D. Hume, "Pope and Swift: Text and Interpretation of Swift's Verses on His Death," *PQ*, 52 (1973), 205–31. Waingrow refutes Slepian acutely and concisely.

48 One supporter of Dr. Slepian's interpretation is Edward Rosenheim, but even Professor Rosenheim has pointed out that "there are certainly observations and sentiments within even the final section of the poem which, whether wistful or savage, must be taken almost literally" (p. 392).

49 This line seems an echo of Martial X.xxx.10, "parcere personis, dicere de vitiis." I wonder what Dr. Slepian would make of the fact. He states that because lines 317–18,

> To steal a hint was never known,
> But what he writ was all his own,

are an echo of Denham's elegy on Cowley, they must be ironical (p. 255).

Slepian points out that Swift commonly lashed or attacked people by name and that he did so in this very poem. But it so happens that Swift produced the same degree of error in his notes, as when he said, "In Ireland the Dean was not acquainted with one single Lord Spiritual or Temporal" (note to line 434). This hyperbole is so gross that it has the effect of a lie; it would also be pointless as irony. One may suppose therefore that both in line 460 and here the heat of rhetoric dissolved the author's sense of proportion, or else one must believe that what is simplicity in the notes is irony in the text.

Several of the statements to which exception is taken spring from the conventions of the genre. To clear his character, the poet employs the traditional apology of satirists. So he identifies his work with general rather than particular satire, and he describes his objects as corrigible. rather than inalterable defects. Hence the echo of Martial (l. 460)—who, incidentally, has also been faulted for misrepresenting his literary character. And hence another couplet that sounds inaccurate:

> His satyr points at no defect,
> But what all mortals may correct.
>
> [ll. 463–64]

Dr. Slepian finds the poem filled with exaggerations—so many, he says, that Swift could not have intended them seriously (p. 254). Now it may indeed be true that all the superlatives, absolutes, and exaggerations of the poem are ironical. But if so, what shall we make of the following passage? It deals with the celebrated pamphlets Dean Swift wrote in opposition to an Englishman's coinage of halfpence and farthings for the Irish people; and if Dr. Slepian is right, Swift here was satirizing his own pride in a famous accomplishment:

> The Dean did by his pen defeat
> An infamous destructive cheat.
> Taught fools their int'rest how to know;
> And gave them arms to ward the blow.
> Envy hath own'd it was his doing,
> To save that helpless land from ruin,
> While they who at the steerage stood,
> And reapt the profit, sought his blood.
>
> [ll. 407–14]

We may believe that in the dozens of lines like these Swift seriously overpraised himself, or we may agree with Dr. Slepian that he dramatically ridiculed himself for being vain.

Dr. Slepian further observes that the style of the poem climbs at points to a sublime—or, rather, quasi-sublime—level that Swift would have repudiated, and he quotes,

Fair LIBERTY was all his cry;
For her he stood prepar'd to die;
For her he boldly stood alone;
For her he oft expos'd his own.

[ll. 347–50]

According to Dr. Slepian, the inflation of language here is meant to poke fun at Swift for exemplifying the same vanity that earlier in the poem he attributed to all mankind. By this device the poet shows himself to be no exception to his own rule (Slepian, p. 256). Dr. Slepian may be right; but if he is, what shall we make of the lines leading up to his quotation and matching it in sonority?

He follow'd David's lesson just,
In princes never put thy trust.
And, would you make him truly sower;
Provoke him with *a slave in power:*
The Irish senate, if you nam'd,
With what impatience he declaim'd!

[ll. 341–46]

In a note Swift explained, "The Irish Parliament are reduced to the utmost degree of slavery, flattery, corruption, and meanness of spirit."[50] Was Swift mocking himself in this note and in the passage it explains? Or did he change without reason and without warning from earnestness to irony, i.e., from serious contempt for the Irish Parliament to ironic praise of his own passion for liberty? Either way, one can hardly describe his art as consummate. If Dr. Slepian is wrong, and all three passages are straightforward, one must still blame Swift for disgusting us by acting as his own flatterer. The question is not, as some critics would suggest, which of these alternatives makes Swift out to be the better poet, but which is the more probable.

What too many critics overlook is that irony as such is not charming. What charms the man with a literary ear is the change from an air of earnestness to a reality of wit, signalizing a change from simplicity to irony. In brilliant irony we expect amusing incongruities of language, plays on words, sarcastic innuendoes, comic deflations of rhetoric, or inversions of points of view. In the widely praised early sections of this poem Swift provided all of these:

In Pope, I cannot read a line,
But with a sigh, I wish it mine:
When he can in one couplet fix
More sense than I can do in six:
It gives me such a jealous fit,
I cry, Pox take him, and his wit.

[ll. 47–52]

[50] *Poems*, ed. H. Williams, 2nd ed. (Oxford: Clarendon, 1958), II, 566, notes.

This is humorous, ironical self-depreciation. If Swift had written so well in the last third of his poem, his vanity would not oppress us. If Dr. Slepian is right, Swift ridiculed himself in both places but did so with zest and wit at the beginning of the poem and with neither at the end. He was for mysterious reasons fumbling in the one passage what he had already shown he could accomplish with elegance in the other.

Literary Meaning

My long tirade against so many works of learning will make me seem reactionary. I must sound as if I wished to reduce the meaning of poetry to its paraphrasable doctrine, as if I condemned every subtle or symbolic interpretation, every disclosure of irony. I have none of these impulses. I ask only that critics and scholars square their exposition of an author's meaning with his explicit statements in the poem they criticize. Reuben Brower has shown how learning, taste, and intelligence can join in the analysis of Pope's allusive style.[51]

I never object a priori to the suggestion that a poet unconsciously rejected what he openly recommends, or that a poet acted in his own life on principles very different from those he embodies in his work. I am always eager to discover the sources of a poet's language or principles. I welcome ironical readings of ironical literature. I realize that doctrine is often the least valuable part of a masterpiece and that meaning is not always explicit.

But I cannot see that origin is the same as meaning or that any mode of discourse, such as the ironic or the allusive, is good in itself, without regard to the use made of it by an author. I believe that some academic critics, in their obsession with coherence and unity—disguised as organic form—have produced a dogma as mischievous as the pseudo-Aristotelian rules. By attributing intrinsic literary value to the machinery of suggestion, they have ignored the whole question of literary judgment; it is remarkable how often they give minute attention to poems or parts of poems that hardly deserve to be read, but which they apparently believe they are endowing with excellence. I cannot see that there is any universal process of creative imagination by which poets of all ages go to work or that the writers I have named Augustan must be shown to exhibit the properties of Mallarmé and Joyce before they gain admission to my pantheon.

[51] *Alexander Pope: The Poetry of Allusion* (Oxford: Clarendon, 1959). Here I cannot keep from praising Professor Brower's less accessible but equally splendid essay, "Form and Defect of Form in Eighteenth-Century Poetry: A Memorandum," in W. H. Bond, ed., *Eighteenth-Century Studies in Honor of Donald F. Hyde* (New York: The Grolier Club, 1970), pp. 365–82.

So I disagree with those critics who befriend Augustan writers by identifying them with modern allusiveness and subversiveness. I am ready to believe that the model used by such admirers is the imagination of post-Symbolist writers, and that many critics wish to treat that imagination as the character of literary genius in all times and all places. Yet I am not sure that allusiveness is the visible hallmark of moderns like Yeats and Frost. I am not sure it is the great feature of Eliot's poetry. Even *The Waste Land* is better off without its notes, better if the macaronic element is treated as unspecified echoes of a decadent culture in a weary, overcivilized mind. I am sure that Eliot in 1933 spoke of his yearning for what D. H. Lawrence before him described as a "stark, bare, rocky directness of statement," and that Eliot went on to say, "This speaks for me of that at which I have long aimed, in writing poetry; to write poetry which should be essentially poetry, with nothing poetic about it, poetry standing in its bare bones, or poetry so transparent that we should not see the poetry, but that which we are made to see through the poetry, poetry so transparent that in reading it we are intent on what the poem *points at*, and not on the poetry."[52] As obbligato to this *cri de coeur* one hears the voice of Wallace Stevens, in his angel of reality: "In my sight, you see the earth again, / cleared of its stiff and stubborn, man-locked set" ("Angel Surrounded by Paysans").

Meanwhile, the relation of statement to suggestion in a poem remains hard to define. But I am troubled when critics speak as if the only job of the one were to ferry us to the other, as if the explicit meaning were somehow exhausted in this journey, after which it withered away and became irrelevant to a new and happier order. Surely the explicit meaning survives as long as the poem is read. If Dryden in *Astraea Redux* exalts Charles II to a Christlike status, the flattery offends us. We may focus our reflections on ideal kingship and shove the historical Charles to one side. But we cannot remove him from the poem, and we cannot remove the poet's distasteful flattery of him. The explicit meaning persists.

If so many excellent scholars have tried to bleach away the explicit element, the cause, I think, is a shell game played with the whole concept of literary meaning. Suppose we consider what an ingenious poet might have had in mind when he wrote a poem: there is one interpretation of a text. If we ask what a subtle reader might infer from the same poem, we get another interpretation. The conventional associations of the words, independent of author and reader, supply a third interpretation. Finally, there are persons, events, facts to which a text refers; these might be studied by themselves and render up a fourth interpretation. Thus a good

[52] Cited by F. O. Matthiessen, *The Achievement of T. S. Eliot,* 2nd ed. (New York: Oxford Univ. Press, 1947), pp. 89–90.

deal of Dryden's reading might have entered into his characterization of Achitophel. A Restoration courtier with a classical education might have found something in the character of Achitophel that Dryden never thought of. The biblical and literary connections of the name Achitophel can be produced without regard to Dryden or a reader of the poem. The historical Earl of Shaftesbury existed in his own right and can as such be brought into the poem.

Yet the meaning of the passages in Dryden's masterpiece that deal with Achitophel seem to me limited by what the author might have expected his reader to find, by what the reader might reasonably attribute to the author, by what either might be expected to know of Achitophel or of Shaftesbury, by what the words of the poem are likely to have meant to Dryden and his audience. If one shifts without noticing from one of my four possibilities to another, the meaning of any poem grows immense. But is not literary meaning determined by what they have in common, rather than the sum of their separate, branching products? Surely, what the author might have had in mind belongs in the poem only insofar as the reader might get it from the words the author used and from the references the reader can identify. Exceptions to this principle exist; the dangers of mechanically applying it are obvious. But in general it seems a safe guide.

Some Values of Explicitness

There is something perverse in the whole effort to distill peculiarly modern features from Augustan literature. Why should one go so far afield for blossoms that crowd about one's feet? Surely if the Augustans can offer only what our contemporaries already possess in bulk, we can survive without them. But I think we are not so well endowed, and that the Augustans not only deviate from us but supply us as well with some distinctly explicit pleasures.

Literary power comes in many kinds. Those who fly from explicit meaning seldom stop at the belief that suggestion is the essence of poetry. They further assume that the wellsprings of suggestion are fresh-packed images and knotty allusions. From such critics we do not often hear of the connotation of true insights, of piercing aphorisms, or of lines like Virgil's "Quae lucis miseris tam dira cupido?" (*Aeneid* VI.721)—in which the reference is not from poetry to poetry or from literal to figurative but from statement to life. Explicitness can mean the undecorated statement of a noble or dreadful truth. Swift wrote about a nation's tolerance of a repressive government, "The Scripture tells us, that *Oppression makes a wise man mad*; therefore, consequently speaking, the reason why some men are not *mad*, is, because they are not *wise*."[53] Johnson wrote about people like himself,

> There mark what ills the scholar's life assail,
> Toil, envy, want, the patron, and the jail.
> [*Vanity of Human Wishes*, ll. 157–58]

In these lines it is syntactic resonance and the reverberations of wisdom that generate depth. The plainness of the expression makes a mordant contrast to the richness of the insight. The reader thinks not of Ecclesiastes or Juvenal but of his own experience of men. This primary power, one of the great strengths of Augustan writers, is seldom noticed even by their admirers today.

Too much care for apothegms or *sententiae* breaks up the continuity of any discourse. This was the complaint of many old critics against the Senecan tradition. In excellent passages of Dryden and Pope one can observe the language rising deliberately from a relaxed flow to an epigram and sinking back again. Halifax holds the reader by a talent for framing his neatest remarks in a lucid context of open but idiomatic relevancies. His terseness catches us as a highlight in a continuity of shimmering depths. When Halifax warned his daughter not to despair over a husband's defects, he wrote,

> I am tempted to say (if the irregularity of the expression could in strictness be justified) that a *wife* is to thank God her *husband* hath *faults*. Mark the seeming paradox my dear, for your own instruction, it being intended no further. A *husband* without *faults* is a dangerous observer; he hath an eye so piercing, and seeth every thing so plain, that it is expos'd to his full censure. And though I will not doubt but that your *vertue* will disappoint the sharpest enquiries; yet few women can bear the having all they say or do *represented* in the clear glass of an understanding without *faults*. Nothing softneth the *arrogance* of our *nature*, like a mixture of some *frailties*. It is by them we are best told, that we must not strike too hard upon others, because we our selves do so often deserve blows: they pull our rage by the sleeve, and whisper gentleness to us in our censures, even when they are rightly applied. The *faults* and *passions* of *husbands* bring them down to you, and make them content to live upon less unequal terms, than faultless men would be willing to stoop to; so haughty is mankind till humbled by common weaknesses and defects, which in our corrupted state contribute more towards the reconciling us to one another, than all the *precepts* of the *philosophers* and *divines*. So that where the *errors* of our *nature* make amends for the *disadvantages* of yours it is more your part to make use of the *benefit*, than to quarrel at the *fault*.[54]

[53] *Prose Works*, ed. H. Davis et al. (Oxford: Blackwell, 1939–68), IX, 18.

[54] George Savile, Marquess of Halifax, *Complete Works*, ed. W. Raleigh (Oxford: Clarendon, 1912), p. 12.

Here, as usual in Halifax's best prose, several diffuse clauses anticipate and move seductively around a concise clause—for example, in the opening sentence, where the last four words balance all the others. The epigram at the beginning of the third sentence echoes so many words in the rest of the paragraph that instead of weakening the other parts, it irradiates them. The whole rhythm of loose and tight depends on the explicitness of the style, without which it could hardly be felt.

In an explicit style, the figures tend to be familiar or easily developed. If the writer uses them simply, in order to foreshadow—or else to follow and illustrate—a remark that is itself clear enough, he can dull the reader's attention. Addison had this bad habit. It is when a writer plays with the relation between one figure and another or between the literal and figurative modes that he begins to charm us. Swift calls an evil man a rat, and calls the king a lion. He believes the man, an ironmonger with a royal patent to mint coins, will ruin Ireland with his coppers; he pretends to believe the king does not realize how evil the man is. Then he writes, "It is no loss of honour to submit to the *lion*: but who, with the figure of a *man*, can think with patience of being devoured alive by a *rat*?"[55] Through their juxtaposition the tired old images grow explosive.

Johnson's faint personifications operate similarly. The personified idea does not merely slip into an explicit sentence. It acts figuratively, and the action itself suggests the meaning of the literal part of the sentence. Often the figure neither illustrates a remark nor is itself unfolded by a parallel remark. Instead, it continues a line of thought that has been started in plain speech. If the figure were fresh and knotty, the effect would be ostentatious; when the figure is commonplace, the effect is charming. To warn a friend against the lure of marriage, Johnson wrote, "There is indeed nothing that so much seduces reason from her vigilance, as the thought of passing life with an amiable woman."[56] The verb "seduces" transforms the faintly personified "reason," making it parallel to the man threatened by matrimony. On the faintness of the personification and the explicitness of the language depend the subtlety of the effect. If the figure were bolder and the language were suggestive, the parallel would turn coarse.

Among the advantages of explicitness is its clarifying of stylistic levels. Augustan authors liked to modulate their verse and prose up and down a scale from the grand or sublime to the humble or plain. If richly figurative speech is kept for the high subjects and characters, the reader can recognize the decorum of that and the other levels and enjoy the movement among them. Dryden controls such effects masterfully in *Aureng-Zebe*, where the Emperor speaks with explicit dignity when the occasion

[55] *Prose Works*, X, 20.

[56] *Letters*, ed. R. W. Chapman (Oxford: Clarendon, 1952), I, 146.

calls for that style but gives way to explicit emotionality during his contests with Nourmahal—especially in Act II, where one can hear the disintegration of his rhetoric.

On lower levels one meets the drama of rational argument. This is not so much a firsthand elaboration of opposed principles as a lively imitation of debate. When Swift, in *The Conduct of the Allies*, or Johnson, in his *Thoughts on . . . Falkland's Islands*, acts out the gestures of persuasive rhetoric, the air of explicitness is fundamental to the reader's satisfaction in following the clearly defined stages of what is in fact a carefully muddled argument.

In literary prose the range of meaningful language and the flexibility of syntax have shrunk since the eighteenth century. We now possess more words but fewer levels of diction; the order of our words is simpler and more rigid. To the vocabulary of literature the real additions have been technical and coarse. We can say "shit" and "cunt," "paraplegia" and "nuclear fission." But the expressive short words are seldom precise; the precise long words are rarely suggestive; and we remain chary of metaphors drawn from chemistry or mathematics. In the works of Joyce, Beckett, and Auden one meets many out-of-the-way words, and they all sound out of the way.

In the eighteenth century the language of theology, logic, metaphysics, and natural science was freely available for figurative use, along with classical mythology—and geography—and the materials of Scripture. At the same time, an elevated, resonant vocabulary could be arranged in a flexible syntax for effects impossible with an explicit style today. In the following quotation from Johnson there are touches of metaphor—the use of Bacchus for wine and the military analogy. These are faded metaphors, whose work depends on their transparent familiarity. If they were strange and striking, the sentence would collapse. Johnson is explaining why Addison's fondness for the company of his intellectual inferiors led him to drink too much: "He that feels oppression from the presence of those to whom he knows himself superior will desire to set loose his powers of conversation; and who that ever asked succour from Bacchus was able to preserve himself from being enslaved by his auxiliary?" ("Addison," in *Lives*, II, 123).

The power of this sentence derives from ingredients hardly available any more. The literal statement appears first; the figurative statement follows, but is neither a parallel nor an illustration. It continues the line of thought, bringing out a surprising implication. There is a quasi-periodic suspension of meaning, thanks to an artificial arrangement of the parts of the sentence; so we are required to pursue a formal, elaborate, balanced design, set apart from colloquial English but carefully explicit. A modern writer is tied to essentially colloquial syntax, to fresh metaphors, to figures that evoke or suggest but do not obviously state. It is because his elements were explicit that Johnson could play with them as he did.

Normally, to appear explicit, one must sound as if one were omitting nothing. The reader must have the impression that the picture, logic, or action is filled in. The writer avoids leaving patterns unfinished. When Pope deals with the five senses in the *Essay on Man*, he runs through all of them, and we expect him to do so, for our pleasure arises from the variety of his examples, epithets, and syntactic shapes. The poet meets the challenge of the pattern he has established, with a richness one could not foresee:

> What modes of sight betwixt each wide extreme,
> The mole's dim curtain, and the lynx's beam:
> Of smell, the headlong lioness between,
> And hound sagacious on the tainted green:
> Of hearing, from the life that fills the flood,
> To that which warbles thro' the vernal wood:
> The spider's touch, how exquisitely fine!
> Feels at each thread, and lives along the line. . . .
>
> [I.211–18]

Addison desired explicitness with continuity. So he habitually finished syntactic patterns while avoiding too neat parallels of rhythm or jingles of sound. He completed analogies and similes; he supplied epithets and connectives. To the need for his kind of coherence he sacrificed aphoristic effects. Therefore, when he indulged in antitheses, he softened them by a lack of rhythmic balance. Hume made this style delightful by the contrast between its smoothness and the startling nature of the doctrines he expounded. Because Addison had no desire to shock, he often grows dull. But when one observes how felicitously he placed the details in order to secure his desiderata, one can only be pleased:

> There is scarce a state of life, or stage in it, which does not produce changes and revolutions in the mind of man. Our schemes of thought in infancy are lost in those of youth; these too take a different turn in manhood, till old age often leads us back into our former infancy. A new title or an unexpected success throws us out of ourselves, and in a manner destroys our identity. A cloudy day or a little sun-shine have as great an influence on many constitutions, as the most real blessings or misfortunes. A dream varies our being and changes our condition while it lasts; and every passion, not to mention health and sickness, and the greater alterations in body and mind, makes us appear almost different creatures. If a man is so distinguished among other beings by this infirmity, what can we think of such as make themselves remarkable for it even among their own species? It is a very trifling character to be one

of the most variable beings of the most variable kind, especially if we consider that he who is the great standard of perfection has in him no shadow of change, but is the same yesterday, to day, and for ever.[57]

In some ways this is at the opposite pole from Pope's style. But as soon as Addison mentioned infancy, we knew he would proceed through all the ages of life. What we didn't know was that instead of ending the pattern with death, he would (like Jaques) choose the more interesting commonplace of a second childhood. The cloudy day requires the alternative of a clear day, but we cannot foresee that Addison's love of asymmetry will couple the first expression with "a little sun-shine." Near the close of the paragraph, the mildly aphoristic phrase, "one of the most variable beings of the most variable kind," foreshadows the close of the paragraph, with its graceful turn in an appropriate but unforeseeable direction and its faintly liturgical cadence.

In their imagery a pervasive charm of the Augustans is the mixture of lucidity with connotation. At the beginning of Eliot's *Prufrock* the famous simile of a patient etherized upon a table produces its effect partly because the structure of the simile breaks with convention. To understand why the evening is like a patient, one must recognize an intermediate stage, the morbid noiselessness of the particular evening, the silence of the lovers. One does not move directly from the figure to its primary meaning, because all evenings are not like this. The definite implication of a quiet evening is obscure; the secondary suggestion of morbidity is clearer. Again, in Hart Crane's line about the dice of dead men's bones (*At Melville's Tomb*) the form of the figure disrupts the usual shape of metaphor because one must grasp the intermediate stage, of bones ground into cubes by the sea, before one can discover the definite implication of the figure. The association of dice with chancefulness is more obvious than the definite implication of bones broken up. A third example is the opening poem in Wallace Stevens's *Harmonium*. Here a mysterious animal called a firecat drives a brush fire which starts and controls the deer. But the brushfire in turn represents the creative imagination, which shapes outer reality. The poet suggests that the imagination must itself be wild or violent if it is to dominate and tame the wilderness of reality. The association of fire imagery with wildness is obvious enough; the definite or primary reference to the imagination is obscure.

But the Augustan preserved the form of the figure, with its definite or primary implication, and relied on the imagery for his vaguer suggestive power. When Swift in *A Tale of a Tub* ridicules the supposed wisdom of shallow journalists, he speaks as one of them, but his imagery shows his contempt for their kind of wisdom:

[57] *Spectator* 162, in *The Spectator*, ed. D. F. Bond (Oxford: Clarendon, 1965), II, 137.

Wisdom is a *fox*, who after long hunting, will at last cost you the pains to dig out: 'Tis a *cheese*, which by how much the richer, has the thicker, the homelier, and the courser coat; and whereof to a judicious palate, the *maggots* are the best. 'Tis a *sack-posset*, wherein the deeper you go, you will find it the sweeter. *Wisdom* is a *hen*, whose *cackling* we must value and consider, because it is attended with an *egg*; But then, lastly, 'tis a *nut*, which unless you chuse with judgment, may cost you a tooth, and pay you with nothing but a *worm*.[58]

The definite implication is clear enough, that wisdom is deep and difficult to get at. But the secondary suggestiveness of the images—fox, maggots, nut, and so on—with their cumulative absurdity still catches at the reader, who hardly notices that the conventional form of the simile has been preserved under this heap of grotesquerie, and who understands that the pretended wisdom is nonsense.

Pope followed the same method in his attack on Sporus (*Epistle to Dr. Arbuthnot*, ll. 305–33). The metaphors require no intermediate state. The reader proceeds directly to their primary implication of evil and hypocrisy. But the suggestive cumulation of butterfly, bug, spaniel, and so on ruins the dignity of Lord Hervey and makes him less frightful than contemptible. In Pope's surface of plain statement and his undertow of powerful suggestion we meet a kind of subtlety that our own age rarely affords.

Finally, there are the many effects of what might be called mock-explicitness. Irony depends on the appearance of saying just what you mean when you are actually withholding the crucial information. In this sense it is Addison's style turned inside out. For example, a common device of excellent ironists is to offer two solutions to a problem as alternatives when both are wrong and a third, apparently rejected by the author, is correct. Hume, in the *Dialogues concerning Natural Religion*, makes great play with this device, representing Cleanthes as nearer the truth than Philo when it is Philo who speaks for the author, and Cleanthes, like Demea, was regarded by Hume as mistaken. The close of this masterpiece is a fine specimen of mock-explicitness: "so I confess, that, upon a serious review of the whole, I cannot but think, that Philo's principles are more probable than Demea's; but that those of Cleanthes approach still nearer to the truth."

In Augustan writing, mock-explicitness takes too many forms to be tabulated. But one of them deserves special notice in light of modern criticism, which busies itself so much with the analysis of images. This is the phenomenon of negative particularity, or the treatment of things unseen or fantastic in rich, explicit detail. Generality so often seems a mark

58 "Introduction," in *Tale of a Tub*, ed. A. C. Guthkelch and D. Nichol Smith, 2nd ed. (Oxford: Clarendon, 1958), p. 66.

of Augustan style that particularity obtrudes itself. In *The False Alarm* Johnson imagines the "progress of a petition" with a minuteness that he never devoted to real events and that is wholly satirical. In *A Journey to the Western Islands* he imagines what the fall of Fiers, dried up by drought, would have looked like in spate: "The river having now no water but what the springs supply, showed us only a swift current, clear and shallow, fretting over the asperities of the rocky bottom, and we were left to exercise our thoughts, by endeavouring to conceive the effect of a thousand streams poured from the mountains into one channel, struggling for expansion in a narrow passage, exasperated by rocks rising in their way, and at last discharging all their violence of waters by a sudden fall through the horrid chasm." (*Fall of Fiers.*)

The humorous charm of the description depends on our understanding that if the author had observed the fall after a spring rain, he would not have described it so particularly. Swift's arithmetical fantasies operate very much like this. In a mania of mock-explicitness he traces the effect of a debased coinage on financial transactions, beginning with the supposed fact that twenty shillings in copper would weigh "six pounds butter weight" and rising systematically (or in Addison's vein) through the classes of wealth to end with one of the richest men in the country: "They say Squire Conolly has *sixteen thousand pounds a year*; now if he sends for his *rent* to town, *as it is likely he does*, he must have *two hundred and fifty horses* to bring up his *half year's rent*, and two or three great *cellars* in his house for stowage. But what the bankers will do I cannot tell. For I am assured, that some great bankers keep by them *forty thousand pounds* in ready cash to answer all payments, which sum in Mr. Wood's money, would require twelve hundred horses to carry it."[59] It would be easy to analyze the details of Parts One and Two of *Gulliver's Travels* as examples of mock-explicitness.

Among the Augustans, concrete particularity was a form of overexplicitness that marked the descriptions of vicious, low, or comic characters. Heroes and sympathetic figures required dignity. They normally received distinct analyses only of their moral constitution: their virtues, motives, affections. For their face, body, or clothing a poet often gave no description or merely relied on general epithets. In Otway's tragedy *The Orphan* a king and a witch are among the people mentioned but never seen. Of the witch, Otway supplies a sensationally vivid and detailed account:

> I spy'd a wrinckled hagg, with age grown double,
> Picking dry sticks, and mumbling to her self;

[59] Letter 1, par. 13, in *The Drapier's Letters*, ed. Herbert Davis (Oxford: Clarendon, 1935), p. 8.

> Her eyes with scalding rhume were gall'd and red;
> Cold palsy shook her head, her hands seem'd wither'd,
> And on her crooked shoulders had she wrapt
> The tatter'd remnant of an old stript hanging,
> Which serv'd to keep her carkass from the cold,
> So there was nothing of a piece about her;
> Her lower weeds were all o're coursely patch'd
> With diff'rent colour'd rags, black, red, white, yellow. . . .
> [II.i.246–55]

But the king's attributes are limited to his virtues:

> He is so good, praise cannot speak his worth;
> So merciful, sure he ne're slept in wrath;
> So just, that were he but a private man,
> He could not do a wrong.
> [II.i.123–26]

The overexplicitness of the witch's portrait suits her lack of dignity.

The link between concrete particularity and satire will be clear to anyone who compares Dryden's catalogue of Shaftesbury's men with that of the royalists in *Absalom and Achitophel.* Swift, in his charming eulogy "To Mrs. Biddy Floyd," contrasts eight virtues possessed by the lady with eight defects that she avoids, but he gives not a word to her appearance. In Pope's second *Moral Essay*, "To a Lady," the representation of vicious women sparkles with concrete imagery; the long celebration of the Lady includes a single reference to blue eyes but otherwise only moral attributes.

One of the pleasures of reading Augustan literature is to observe how style thus reflects a view of human nature. To define the virtues and even beauty, the author seemed equipped with public standards, commonly recognized, which he could indicate with easy efficiency. Ugliness, affectation, low life, and vice seemed more various and surprising, and therefore more suitable for concrete particularity.

If one glances now at the genre that most directly joins us to the Augustans, viz. the novel, one observes similar phenomena. In the systematic fictions, the sham autobiographies, histories, and documents of Defoe, Fielding, and Richardson, we often fail to meet concrete particularity just where we might expect it—as in Fielding's refusal to describe the heroine of *Tom Jones* when she makes her entrance. Often we do meet it in fantasies, as when Lovelace imagines Clarissa as an infatuated mistress.[60]

These distinctions return us to the center of my case, the plea that in shortening the space between the Augustans and ourselves we should not deprive them of the color of their difference. The lack of concrete par-

[60] Samuel Richardson, *Clarissa*, Everyman's Library, II, 251–52.

ticularity where we are used to it results perhaps from the same cause as the supply of negative particularity where we don't look for it. What is truly seen in our own literature today has to be seen through the impressions of a unique sensibility. For us the realities that count in literature are embodied in radically private experience. For the Augustans the important truths were shared truths. What had to be rendered in bright detail was what did not belong to the familiar things of their world. What mattered to them, therefore, was what could be communicated. This finally is why they made such refreshing and inventive use of explicit modes of speech.

II. *Personae*

In an age when the nature of human identity has been examined by new and alarming procedures with new and alarming results, it is proper that we should interpret the monuments of literature as embodying that preoccupation. The works of many modern authors owed their conception to the same interests that directed the philosophers and psychologists. Quite spontaneously, therefore, the attempt to pursue such questions in literary studies began with contemporary reviews or studies of these authors. In the masks of Yeats and the autoanalysis of Proust's Marcel or Joyce's Bloom appeared poetic structures like the laminating egos that fascinated Freud and William James. Very soon, the gains accruing from such criticism of modern authors encouraged scholars to try parallel methods in historical research.

About this time, several young critics had also begun to enlarge their powers of interpretation by applying to one genre the terms developed for the study of another. Thus modern lyric poems found themselves treated as small dramas, modern novels as poems. When scholars again followed the procedures of these brave innovators, we had Shakespearean tragedy presented in the categories commonly reserved for lyric poetry and epics considered as tragedies.

The fruitful effect of these methods of dealing with literature has transformed what once threatened to be an increasingly sterile labor into the most adventurous of humanistic pursuits. Nevertheless, such methods, like any other way of disengaging the various elements that constitute a masterpiece, can never create values but can only reveal them. They can be applied as easily, therefore, in the support of entrenched opinion as in the establishment of new judgments. The former is what I think has sometimes occurred in the mingling of these rhetorical methods for the interpretation of works belonging to the age of Pope and Swift. Certain prejudices have been propped up by skillful carpentry instead of undergoing the probing that they deserve.

Yet these prejudices in turn were the outcome of an honest effort to rescue the Augustans from imprisonment in old Romantic commonplaces: Elwin's Pope, Thackeray's Swift, enacting mythical scandals before voyeurist literary societies. To effect the rescue, the scholars reversed the Romantic momentum and established an ideal of impersonal art as the distinguishing property of these writers. The *Essay on Man*, for example, became not a statement of Pope's own impressions but a reflection of traditional wisdom distinct from the beliefs or disbeliefs of the poet.

So successful did the first rescuers feel that later salvage operations were mounted for the more remote parts of the authors' *œuvre*. Invoking now the principles of rhetoric to account for poetic effects and the emanations of a multiplied consciousness to account for apparently direct self-expression, a number of subtle, erudite scholars found impersonal art where it was earlier thought to be inaccessibly submerged.

The main instrument for these researches has been an elusive idea, rarely defined, which represents the compounding of two tendencies sketched above. In this compound, the terms of one genre are applied to another: narrative fiction is treated as drama; the didactic essay is treated as narrative fiction; lyric, didactic, and narrative poetry are treated as drama or rhetoric. To supply characters or debating sides for the story, play, or dialogue, the consciousness of the creator is divided up. Where a work once seemed to be the expression of an author's feelings or views, the scholars can separate the various tones heard in it and incarnate each as implying a change of speaker. Sometimes, more simply, the reader becomes a part of the action, and the work becomes a type of persuasive speech organized so as to alter his opinion; a *façon de parler* is transformed into an essential structure.

For almost a quarter-century, the concept thus constructed has been finding wider and wider employment in research dealing with Swift, Pope, and their contemporaries. To produce the concept now is to mark oneself as furnished with a sharp critical method. Most scholars call it "persona" or "mask," but other labels are to be found. Rhetoricians speak of "ethical judgment" or "ethos." Exegetical critics may prefer "implied dramatic speaker." All those who like the method of study based on this concept seem to believe that if the structure of a poem involves a persona, the work deserves special praise on that account.

Although terminology may vary, the concept as normally invoked seems to imply certain common presuppositions. Fundamental is the principle that a literary work should be regarded not as an aspect of the author's personality but as a separate thing. As a consequence, the sentiments expressed in a literary work are not to be attributed to the author himself. In the room of the author, one is well advised to lodge an intermediate figure, the speaker or narrator created by him. It is to this persona that we may then assign the attitudes which seem implicit in a literary work. The persona again is not to be considered an aspect or revelation of the author but an independent creation, designed for its function as part of the self-contained work. The use of a persona by a writer is thus a mark of talent, a sign by which we may distinguish superior from mediocre achievement. In the critic, similarly, the method that concentrates on the persona is a sign of analytic skill. For any reader at all, an awareness of this concept will quicken his appreciation of a literary masterpiece. Or so (by implication) we are told.

The whole ground on which the search for the persona is based seems to me the belief that it is a device of art, that it belongs to the realm of peculiarly literary talent. There would be no profit in the attempt to identify it in imaginative literature if it were merely an inseparable part of language and communication; we do not praise an author for using participial phrases. Yet I believe that the persona or mask, as usually employed, has no status as art in itself, unless we admit such art to be congenital in humankind.

Thus, reasoning a fortiori, I should say the most subtle expression of the concept is that in which, according to the critic, an author pretends to be himself but acts a calculated role: Pope, for instance, in *An Epistle to Dr. Arbuthnot.* In so doing, the author—we are assured—gives his true name and supplies reliable information about his life. He suppresses or even distorts some of his honest views, however, so that the opinions and data presented in the work contribute to a rhetorical purpose; they do not necessarily conform with his private conversation or with his actual behavior. By this device, the author draws a public portrait, to be used on public occasions. It is argued that only a novice among scholars would confuse the portrait with the man.

Yet it seems that this kind of rhetorical pose is absolutely inseparable from all language and communication. One could never reveal the whole truth about oneself, even supposing one knew it. If one could, the effect would be chaos, for to reveal all is to hide all. One cannot speak without selecting a limited number of remarks from among possible remarks, and it is animal instinct to choose those which suit the occasion. A hound growls confidently at a spaniel but slinks without noise beside its own trainer. Children have the same talent, varying their characters according to the adult whom they must govern.

In every conversation, we misrepresent our nature. To the degree that the speaker in the *Epistle to Dr. Arbuthnot* does not stand for Alexander Pope, no man, in a single speech, can be wholly himself. If the effect produced by a speech gives a misleading or one-sided image of the speaker, the reason is that to be coherent one must expose one side at a time. Misrepresentation in the vulgar sense is no issue in literary art. As audience, we try to discover what the real author means in the particular work. That he may possibly (without our knowing) deliver a different doctrine elsewhere, or that his life may exemplify the vices he begs us to avoid, is irrelevant. At the moment, in the poem, he says what we have to accept as his assertion if no evidence appears to the contrary.

To argue otherwise is to make the author defy the polite rules of language. We customarily hear a man's speech as revealing his character in the same way that his gestures and actions do. Communication is impossible on any other basis. So long as there is no hint of deceitfulness, what a man says must be precisely what he means. In suggesting that we are not to take Pope at his word when he makes a statement in a poem, an essay, or a private letter, the critic is turning a genius into a fool. It is inconceivable that a writer as sensitive to overtones as Pope should deliver a proposition from his own lips and expect the reader to doubt that he feels responsible for it. Where, on the other hand, we find suggestions that the speech is ironical, or that the reasoning is suspended, or that a remark was intended to trick a specific correspondent, an intelligent reader will, of course, take warning from the cues.

For instance, it is sometimes argued that we are wrong to read the description of Sporus as the author's judgment on the historical Hervey; rather, we are told, it represents the imagined satirist-speaker's detestation of an example of evil. Such an analysis leaves Pope a pathetic fumbler. If it should hold, the poet would have described Hervey in epithets that force us to recall Queen Caroline's confidant; he would have endowed his own voice with the most vindictive harshness; yet he would have desired us to shut our ears to these thunderclaps and follow only the light patter of his pseudo-rhetorical design. True, the character of Sporus does erupt at an appropriate point in the poem; true, Hervey's career is treated by Pope as a type of radical evil; true, we are indebted to those scholars who demonstrated that far from expressing an odd fit of malice, the character has a significant position in a moral structure. But even more truly, in these verses we hear Pope attacking Hervey.

If there is any meaning in the concept of persona or mask it must imply a difference between appearance and reality. The mask of Yeats is not the true Yeats; the "citizen" who wrote Defoe's *Journal* is not really Defoe. Inevitably, the term implies that a genuine person does exist, could reveal himself, but chooses not to. It implies that while the work of the person is solid to the touch, it is not only distinguishable from him but essentially different from him. The more freely the term is employed, the more remote grows the being who lives behind its fence. Huckleberry Finn is not Mark Twain, who is not Samuel Clemens. By similar logic, even the speaker or narrator of a work is not traceable to the author but is a detached expression of his creative sensibility; and indeed any connection between the sensibility and the mask is haphazard.

Surely one appeal of these principles is that as artists Yeats, Defoe, and

Clemens retain an extraordinary integrity throughout the operation of the method. Inept or distasteful aspects of their work can always be interpreted as revelations of the character of the "speaker," while the author remains deft and refined. Conrad, not to be confused with Marlow, can be anchored like the tortoise who supports the elephant on which the world rests. The more admiring but defensive we feel toward an author, the more reassurance we draw from this knowledge.

In studying the Augustans, an emphasis on masks offers us the special advantages of guarding their reputation for impersonality and eluding the charge of boastfulness. As it happens, Swift, Pope, Dryden, and Defoe often spoke out boldly and directly. *Gulliver's Travels* is abundantly supplied with passages in which Swift gave the reader a piece of his mind, as when he denounced the English voters of his day for prostituting themselves by accepting bribes (III.viii). Pope's greatest powers appear in a work like the *Epilogue to the Satires*, which could not be more direct without turning ink to acid. But if we wish to ignore the violence of expression in such works and hunt only for a device to screen the author from his meaning, we may rouse up the concept of persona. Committed to the dogma of impersonal art, we may dismiss every evidence to the contrary as an attribute of the speaker alone; and having set this evidence aside, we may at last treat the poem as one more demonstration of Augustan impersonality.

By means of the same strategy, we can also dissipate the aura of vainglory that floats about any defense of one's own career. When an author displays his moral virtue in public, he can scarcely avoid opening himself to the charge of vanity. *The Life and Genuine Character of Dr. Swift* embarrasses many of the Dean's admirers by its undertone of self-approbation. This poem came out less than two years before *An Epistle to Dr. Arbuthnot* and bore a long dedication to Pope, who may even have been involved in its publication. Because it also deals with the same autobiographical themes as the later work, I think Pope may have had it in mind when he was composing the *Epistle*. Certainly he committed the same blunder, for if Pope's poem remains a masterpiece, it does so in spite of the self-praise hinted in many lines. Once again, however, by introducing the persona and classifying the poetry as rhetoric, we can claim that not the author but the speaker is responsible for the praise and that his object is not Pope but the ideal satirist, the poet's so-called ethos.

Thus a further source of gratification is the analogy between artistic integrity and moral integrity. If the literary manifestation of a man may be isolated from the man, so may his nonliterary expression. Just as the narrator of the *Plague Year* is not Defoe, so also one might claim that the author of the obsequious letters to Oxford represents not so much Defoe as a pose assumed for the statesman by the journalist. Similarly, whatever insinuation Pope may have written to Warburton against Swift, we may now deny that the attitude tells anything about the real Alexander Pope, for the remark could have been intended strictly to impress his correspondent. As we advance along these routes, language generally is transformed from a means of communication into a means of deceit and concealment. All that appears as the expression of a man's feelings is available for analysis as the artful construction of a masked genius. Through such casuistry, however, not only is the literary status of a man's work enhanced, but his moral rectitude is barricaded.

Perhaps we are still further consoled by this critical method because it inferentially secures the integrity of our own characters. By treating ourselves as we do the authors, we may sacrifice every appearance to preserve the essence. In any regrettable act, we can say, "This is not the real me; my essential good nature remains hidden but genuine." During an age when the notion of the self is collapsing like the notion of the soul, the concept of persona enables us to cling a little longer to a substantial ego. For the glittering charm of the concept resides in its never leading us toward the issue but always sending us in the opposite direction. So quietly does it take for granted the pure self, isolated and idealized, that we fail to observe the existence of an assumption.

In such rationalizations, there would be little charm if we abandoned the postulate of an essence distinct from all its manifestations, if we admitted that not only communication but personality is impossible apart from learned, conventional behavior—"poses," if you like. When there is no audience, we act for ourselves. We cannot think or even dream without "posing." As long as a man's character is alive, it is trying out roles in language, in conduct. At the same time, although one "self" does continually displace another, each remains a form or mode of revelation of the real person. It is not illusory appearances that the real person sets before us; it is visible effluences, aspects, reflections—however indirect—of an inner being that cannot be defined apart from them. In order to understand any literary work, we must view it as a transaction between us and that inner being. If he tells a story, we must ask what he (not his emanation) means by the story; if he writes a play, we must ask what he intended to express through its action; if he talks by way of an intermediary figure, we must ask how he uses the intermediary; if he sounds ironical, we must discover the direct sense implied by the irony.

Among the several benefits conferred upon a poem by the kind of rhetorical analysis that focuses itself on a persona, the most seductive is the apparent improvement in the merits of the work. This improvement is discovered first in the alleged appropriateness of the speaker to the design and second in the alleged persuasiveness of the reasoning. About forty-five years ago, John Brooks Moore mistakenly described Gulliver as "an entirely credible and probable person at the same time that he is precisely the person to enforce Swift's demonstration."[1] Gulliver is none of these things, but Moore's comment foreshadowed similar judgments by other scholars on a wide range of Pope's and Swift's works. In each case, the brief follows the same line. We are told what the implicit purpose of the poem or essay is. We are then told what qualities an orator should possess if he is to execute the purpose. Finally, we are shown that the mask or persona employed exhibits just these traits and no others. *The Essay on Criticism*, the Digressions of *A Tale of a Tub*, the *Epistle to Bathurst*, the *Drapier's Letters*—all have rung true to this elaborate test.

What the analyst fails to notice is the source of his standard of judgment. In order to determine the implicit purpose of, say, *An Epistle to Dr. Arbuthnot*, one must examine the attitudes and sentiments of the speaker of the poem. From the clues contained therein, we find that it is a piece of argument intended by a high-minded poet to refute the accusations of his dishonest enemies. The purpose of the speech is the rehabilitation of the poet's character; the speech must prove the justice of his past actions to an audience that sits on the bench. Pope himself tells us as much, directly and covertly, in his verses. If we now examine the character of the persona, we see, naturally enough, that he is a high-minded author, harassed beyond patience by a gang of dishonest enemies. This is the ideal figure to speak the bill of complaint that constitutes the poem.

Transparently, such an analysis carries us around in a circle. If we deduce the intention of a poem from the attitudes implicit in the sentiments of the poet, we shall inevitably discover that the speaker of the poem has sentiments appropriate to its purpose. So long as intention and character are but different aspects of the same data, there is no breaking the circle.

But the rhetorical analysis moves on, to praise the argument of the poem as such. As before, the operation hinges upon the separation of the speaker from the author, for we could not regard the *Epistle* as an artful structure of persuasive devices if we left it in the category of a self-revelation. Once this split is accomplished, the connection of the poem with history is destroyed. Because its purpose is not to tell the truth but to appear truthful, the advocate must be divided from the defendant.

I have already suggested that if such an approach is valid, Pope was inept, because the speaker of the *Epistle* appeals continuously to history, resting his defense upon the verifiable truth of his data. Now this appeal seems to me anterior to the surface of rhetorical persuasion. If the author of this poem were not the great poet of his age, if his relations with his parents were not well known to have been as he testified, if Atticus and

[1] "The Rôle of Gulliver," *MP*, 25 (1928), 469.

Sporus did not belong to public life, the force of the poem would dwindle.

I may further suggest that even the pseudo-rhetorical framework in which the poet chose to deliver his self-defense belongs less to the realm of persuasive discourse than to the tradition of poetry. The "bill of complaint" form, of course, descended to Pope not from Aristotle's *Rhetoric* but from Horace. Between Pope's *Epistle* and such works of Horace as his *Satires* I.iv, the parallels are so close that we may regard the Latin poems as authority for the English poem's structure.

The *Epistle to Dr. Arbuthnot* is cast in the form of a dialogue, and a persuasive line of reasoning has always been evident in it. But until recently, this form was assumed to be a *façon de parler*, a lucid figure of speech, allowing the poet to vary his point of view and to avoid monotony. Nobody took it any more literally than the stroll-through-a-studio setting of *An Epistle to a Lady*. It was never doubted that the voice heard within the long speeches came from the throat of Pope himself. If we deny this principle and handle the surface of rhetoric as the essential form, we drive ourselves into the paradox I have already described; the poem must then be understood as irrelevant to the history and character of Pope, yet uttered by a speaker with his identity.

The benefits derived from this unnatural attitude are indeed great. Not only do we block, as extraliterary, any effort to interpret the poem as evidence of Pope's own sensibility. We also transform it into a flawless piece of ratiocination. The cause of this will be obvious. Every attempt to persuade a listener of the truth of a proposition involves not only the correct marshaling of logic, data, or sentiments but also a claim of truthfulness that can be judged by nothing but a reference to reality. If we classify a speech as rhetoric and in it, at the same time, refuse to admit any allusion to reality, we allow a man to prove a case by inventing whatever facts will support his demonstration; we free him from the responsibilities of rhetoric and endow him with the privileges of poetic. If in addition to these licenses, the debater possesses great eloquence, he will of course compose a masterpiece of argument. In the particular instance of the *Epistle to Dr. Arbuthnot*, as it happens, the argument itself urges us to look at the facts as verifiable. So we can ignore that element only by distorting the whole meaning of the speech.

As a specimen of imaginative art, the *Epistle*, therefore, is not simply rhetoric but an imitation of rhetoric. Like all Pope's satires in this form, it has a rhetorical scaffolding, but this is not the inner edifice. Yet even the light framework can be irritating. To the degree that we regard the verses not as complex poetry but as simple persuasion, we must feel annoyed by several flaws: by the fallacies in the poet's logic, by the improbable helpfulness of the questions planted in the friend's mouth, by the astonishing ease with which the friend accepts the poet's conclusions, by the unfair advantage that the poet grants his own intellect over his sympathizer's. When, however, we regard the pseudo-rhetorical form as a conventional means of giving life to the speaker-poet's expression of his own views, we moderate our annoyance and admire the art.

True, it would be absurd to read the whole of this poem, or the imitations of Horace, or the autoanalytical poems of Swift and Prior, as direct, literal statements of the author's principles. It is equally a mistake to read them as independent of those principles. Through his masterpieces a man defines—not hides—himself. By reading them, we are put in touch with him, not with a series of intermediaries. The nature of his communication may be subtle; his manner, devious. Ultimately, however, he is telling us his truth. If we about must and about must go, it is in order to reach that, and not some beautiful, self-contained, illusory Helen.

I think it would be a service to literature to distinguish the helpful from the misleading applications of the persona in methods of scholarship and criticism. The least illuminating applications seem those which treat mere personae as full, interesting characters. Swift's pseudonyms, for example, are sometimes treated this way; and yet they rarely depend on self-consistent, rounded figures. Except when he used what may be called the "ironical persona," Swift ignored the pseudonym and its few attached facts; in the body of the work, he spoke in his own way (ironical or direct), expounding his own views. In the creation of Gulliver, Swift cannot be recommended for consistency either of character or of fact. Again and again the veneer of probability is broken.

Broadly it can be said, on the other hand, that the most illuminating applications are made to works whose structure depends on the speaker's having an ambiguous character. I have claimed that any communication involves a kind of pose. But when this necessity is itself manipulated so as to become a method of communicating attitudes otherwise unacceptable to the reader, the result is a special form of art, the "ironical persona." I use this to designate a disguise that is intended to be seen through, a mask that the reader at first supposes to be genuine but at last sees removed. In such a literary structure, the author's fundamental tone also reverses itself; what sounded sober is transformed to mockery. For the device to succeed, the reader must be tricked during the early stages of the work and be undeceived during the later, and in his gradual apprehension of the meaning of the work, the process that removes the disguise must provide a dramatic turning point. Swift's *Modest Proposal* is an example.

The art of the employer of the ironical mask springs from his power to combine ambiguous moral sentiments with an ambiguous attitude toward what he is saying. The reader must assume that the doctrines to be expounded are proper, decent things. He must also assume that the author is serious in proposing them. The skill of the writer appears in his disclosing the wickedness of the doctrines before disclosing the irony of his manner. The longer the reader can be kept in suspense between the two revelations, the sharper is the effect. The greater the degree of fascinated ambivalence that results, the greater is the achievement of the satirist.

This effect, in turn, depends on the fact that we naturally sympathize with any speaker who sounds calm and well intentioned. It is a mistake to think that the skill of the author, in these maneuvers, should be measured by the ease with which he first leads the reader into associating himself with the speaker; for it is the instinctive, nonliterary tendency for all readers or listeners to commit themselves to the side of an unknown author, merely by embarking upon the effort of following a speech or essay. A persona need not be peculiarly designed to make the reader identify himself with the author; it need only be neutral enough not to discourage what amounts to a natural impulse. It would not matter whether Gulliver were a physician or a merchant, whether he studied at Emmanuel College, Cambridge, or Brasenose, Oxford, so long as none of his features were likely to alienate the sympathy of the reader.

In the opening sections of the work, the reader assumes, therefore, that the moral character of the speaker is essentially like his own, and in this sense he identifies the two. What the man in the ironical mask must attempt is to retain this sympathy after the reader has contemplated the evil or absurdity of the recommendations. While, then, the reader is struggling to disengage his fellow feeling—that is, while he still feels reluctant to admit that he was wrong to give a fair hearing to the author—it must grow obvious that the author himself is not in earnest but is delivering a parody, acting out a caricature of a type of man he loathes or contemns. The effect on the reader is double, for he sees himself derided by the very person he has been straining to respect. At the same time, he feels that the author, by taking his initial sympathy for granted, has pinned the loathsome character on him. In fact, it is because of this sympathy that he is being ridiculed. If the maneuver is successful, the reader cannot help exerting himself to reject the character.

This sort of ironical mask has become a familiar prop in the theater of modern criticism. Not only have we seen it fall from the face of Swift's Projector; we have watched a series of dressers trying to fit it over the face of Lemuel Gulliver. More insight than confusion, certainly, has emerged from these analyses. Yet I think they often suffer from an extension of the error associated above with the idea of a rhetorical pose, that is, the detachment of appearance from essence.

Scholars dealing with the ironical mask often assume that whenever it drops, the author remains hidden; only the speaker or narrator is revealed. Behind the sensible Projector's advice there suddenly looms a monster, but behind the monster the author stands allegedly undefined. I believe, on the contrary, that *A Modest Proposal* makes sense only if we treat the voice as the author's throughout. Swift is so ambiguous that at first we think he is in earnest. At the moment of understanding, we realize that he has been speaking in parody. There is no intermediate person between the real author and us. Surely the inference we draw when a decent, intelligent man produces an abominable scheme is that he doesn't mean it, that he is ironical, that he speaks in parody. Surely we read the *Modest Proposal* as a wildly sarcastic fantasy delivered by the true author, whoever he may be. Surely the kind of literary disguise that is deliberately intended to be penetrated is a method of stating, not hiding, what one thinks.

As it happens, Swift corroborates this interpretation by using a third style in the essay, the mode of direct, bitter statement (like the vituperations that grow thick and frequent toward the end of *Gulliver's Travels*). To such outbursts both the noncommittal and ironic modes give way—in *A Modest Proposal*—when Swift says the landlords of Ireland have devoured the parents of the poor, or when he cuttingly attacks the frivolous young ladies, or when he lists real remedies for the condition of Ireland, or when he says England would gladly eat up the whole Irish nation. To maintain the hypothesis of an intermediate figure, one would have to claim either that the projector himself grows ironic in these passages or else that a third, angry person exists, creating an abominable projector who pretends to be a humane patriot.

Instead of multiplying entities so liberally, I suggest that we deal at once with the satirist. Whether or not he cracks the surface of the irony, an ironical hoaxer must show himself if his device is to succeed. Behind the author of the *Guardian* No. 40, on pastorals, the discriminating reader must meet not a silly critic blind to his own lacklogic but a detester of Philips and an admirer of Pope. In ordinary conversation, when an intelligent friend suddenly utters absurdities in a sober tone, we do not conclude that he has changed his identity but that he is using deadpan irony. If his wit grows so mocking that he seems to be imitating a particular fool or type of fool, we do not imagine that he has been metamorphosed. Surely we can deal as reasonably with a literary impersonation.

In all speech, literary or nonliterary, it is as meaning only that there can be perceptible form. The primacy of meaning does not originate or end in the rhetorical persuasiveness of the speaker. It does not depend on our agreement or disagreement with him. Rather it springs from the power of his case to arouse us to intense contemplation one way or the other.

Whether we say that the argument seems worth resisting, or we feel that it is the voice of our own mind, the meaning remains effective. If an author moves us to fight against his doctrines, he may have lost as a rhetorician, but he has won as a poet. It is when we feel that the case is worth neither entertaining nor refuting that the speech is negligible.

Only as a relationship between a real speaker and a real listener can meaning exist. In drama and prose fiction or epic, where separate speeches illustrate separate characters, the whole narrative must be read as a parable whose implications can be gathered from the light in which the various elements appear. The author is speaking this parable to the audience. In didactic or lyric poetry, as in the reflective or polemical essay, the author must be regarded as the speaker. He may talk ironically; he may imitate a man he despises; he may ask you to sneer at the fool he is copying; he may in mockery talk like his foolish audience. But unless we treat the material as indicating, however indirectly, what the author believes and is, we do not discover the meaning of the work; and if we miss its meaning, we cannot judge its form.

Part Two

Some Applications

III. *The Style of Sound*

The Literary Value of Pope's Versification

In the academic criticism of poetry no standard of merit seems accepted more instinctively than the accommodation of sound to sense. If a poet makes his meter suggestive of his meaning, he is bound to be praised. A particular feature commonly admired is what might be called "local expressiveness," or the apparent matching of rhythms and sounds within a line or couplet to the meaning of the words themselves. This well-defined accomplishment I distinguish from a general decorum or propriety of style, such as the use of sharp stresses for the speech of an angry man or the adoption of a leisurely stanza for a quiet verse tale. It is not, in other words, a broad congruence of style with character or action. Instead, it is the more localized effect, such as the crowding of heavy consonants into a line about climbing a hill or a repetitious series of vowels in a line about echoes.

The judicial exaltation of these devices goes along with the unexamined presumption that they do not undermine other literary merits, i.e., that they happily enrich the texture of a poem regardless of its genre or mode. Whether a passage happens to be narrative or expository, eulogistic or insulting, dignified or comic, we seem implicitly advised that expressive or imitative effects can only add positive value. Unobtrusively, they have taken over the position once held by purely musical qualities, and they still surpass in prestige those qualities of dramatic speech which have got wider and wider appreciation in the last twenty years. From local expressiveness flow theoretical benefits to the rhetoric, the beauty, and the truth of a poem.

Of course, the vaguer sort of pervasively decorous versification hardly escapes the notice of learned observers. If a poem modulates ingeniously from a rich, slow pattern of vowels and pauses to a dry, irregular pattern, when a boy's death is followed by a mourner's despair, most critics rejoice with analytic praise. So deep is the identification of this aspect of style with self-evident value that the workaday critic is satisfied merely to demonstrate the devices, without considering whether they may not deserve more blame than approval. Once the phenomena are visible, their merit is settled. Rarely does one find a line drawn between better and worse types of expressive or imitative technique.

Pope has received unusual applause for such accomplishments. In the

Pastorals Joseph Warton found little to recommend besides their "correct and musical versification." Robert K. Root celebrated the "infinite metrical riches within the little room of twenty syllables."[1] More recent scholars and critics have carried the examination of Pope's "style of sound" to the point of electronic microscopy.

Yet I find that, except in a few masterpieces, Pope made large sacrifices in order to secure his beauties, and I suspect it must always be so. For instance, a devotion to expressive effects relieves an author from more profound demands of structure, whether narrative or expository. A series of discrete items lends itself to aural refinements as a well-told story or coherent argument does not. In the *Ode for Musick*, the *Essay on Criticism*, and the *Dunciad* we see instructive examples of this principle. Throughout a passage in the *Ode* like

> Dreadful gleams,
> Dismal screams,
> Fires that glow,
> Shrieks of woe,
> Sullen moans,
> Hollow groans

the order of details is not only insignificant but also grotesque. If the sharply contrasted vowels and heavy pauses do indeed suggest the cries and pangs of souls in Hades, the poet's indifference to any other considerations makes the lines sound like a deliberately inane parody. In another part of the *Ode for Musick*, as Warton pointed out, the metrical form is hilariously incongruous. Orpheus has rescued Eurydice, and Pope says,

> Thus song could prevail
> O'er death and o'er Hell,
> A conquest how hard and how glorious?
> Though Fate had fast bound her
> With Styx nine times round her,
> Yet musick and love were victorious.

The choice and treatment of the feet suggest triumph and release, either through the shifts from short to long lines or else through the sonority and vigor of the suddenly feminine rhymes—the first feminine rhymes in the poem. But of course, the rhythms are so quick, heavy, and abrupt that they suggest not solemn rejoicing but farce. In the fifth stanza a progression of images is hinted at: from the inanimate, through plantlife, to human beings. Yet the poet's obsession with vowels, rhymes, and pauses makes the choice of details seem pointlessly capricious: streams, winds,

[1] Warton, *Essay on Pope* (London, 1806), I, 9; Root, *The Poetical Career of Alexander Pope* (Princeton Univ. Press, 1938), p. 50.

flowers; souls, meads, bowers; heroes, youths, Eurydice. Again Pope sacrificed the pull of narrative or exposition to the advantage, for his narrow purpose, of a disorderly collection of specimens.[2]

In the *Essay on Criticism* the famous "echo to the sense" passage is less deplorable, mainly because it is explicitly illustrative and the poet does not pretend to supply a structure of persuasive rhetoric. If the passage were short, it would still be oppressive, since the effects are coarse and showy. But only a comic design could redeem the length of forty lines consecrated to a display of easy art. Johnson's complaint may be irrelevant when he says in effect that most impressions of sound conveying sense are imaginary: yet I find it significant that he quoted as "one of the most successful attempts" two couplets not by Pope but by Broome.[3] If one supposes *r* to be an effortful noise, it requires little genius to crowd a line with *r*'s—though even in his youth Pope knew enough to avoid excessive alliteration here. The alexandrine snake and the line about monosyllables sink lower yet, and for all their fluent precision and idiomatic effectiveness, they only serve as crashingly obvious examples. Contrariwise, some couplets in the passage exhibit not local expressiveness but a more subtle decorum of sound, and these allow Pope's true gifts to appear:

> praise the *easie vigor* of a line,
> Where Denham's strength and Waller's sweetness join.
> [ll. 360–61]

Even taking such moments into account, I think the disjunctive, miscellaneous nature of the images deprives the passage of real grace and charm. Not that all my complaints together can relegate this long paragraph to the same level as the *Ode for Musick*. There are too many agreeable subtleties in it, such as the elegant transitions from point to point, or the natural grouping of observations within the whole sequence, or the gradual approach to the brilliant, climactic ending. It represents a step up.

For the most magnificent sacrifice of coherence to local expressiveness we can look at the last stage of Pope's career. In the *Dunciad* of 1743, when Dulness watches the breeding of new theatrical entertainments, Pope delivers ten couplets with almost no anchorage (I.59–78). Zembla's fruits could change places with Barca's flowers if it were not for the rhyme; "hoary hills" and "painted vallies" are equally reversible. The

[2] The musical setting may have compensated for the effects I find; but of course this poem, like Dryden's similar poems, was published by the author; the odes of both poets have been praised by modern critics as independent literary works. Handel's operas illustrate what a great composer can do with puerile materials.

[3] *Lives of the English Poets*, ed. G. B. Hill (Oxford: Clarendon, 1905), III, 231.

vocabulary of "how," "here," and "there" calls our attention to the floating interchangeability of the parts:

> How tragedy and comedy embrace;
> How farce and epic get a jumbled race. . . .

The entire passage of twenty lines fits no better where Pope left it than it would two paragraphs earlier with

> Hence hymning Tyburn's elegiac lines,
> Hence Journals, Medley's, Merc'ries, Magazines.

It's no good reflecting that Pope meant to describe chaos and chaos is disorderly. We can do with a very short evocation of simple disorder. What the artist has to produce is a shapely expression of unshapely material, just as he must contrive to make boredom interesting. But again and again the *Dunciad* breaks up into lists of specimens, like the catalogue of Cibber's books, or the file of scribblers falling asleep:

> At last Centlivre felt her voice to fail,
> Motteux himself unfinish'd left his tale,
> Boyer the state, and Law the stage gave o'er,
> Morgan and Mandeville could prate no more. . . .
>
> [II.411–14]

It would be misleading to imply that a single motive could account for the atomization of the *Dunciad*. Pope had many witty turns he wished to show off in the poem, and most of them fit more easily into a collection of detached lines than a tightly organized march of ideas. Among the tricks of the last quotation above is the ripple of names growing out from a center: first one name to a line, then two, and then three—"Norton, from Daniel and Ostraea sprung." Another refinement is the matching of the rhyme words "o'er" and "more" to the names Boyer, Morgan, and Norton. Often in the poem we notice how much Pope loved the effect of anticlimax at the end of a parade of apparently similar items; so at the beginning of Book III he lists some products of false inspiration:

> Hence the fool's paradise, the statesman's scheme,
> The air-built castle, and the golden dream,
> The maid's romantic wish, the chemist's flame,
> And poet's vision of eternal fame.
>
> [III.9–12]

Ironically bowing in his own direction, Pope ends the sequence with humorous bathos. Clearly, such accomplishments—and I have only sampled the many varieties—discourage an author from trying to establish a large, unified design.[4]

[4] One might argue that local expressiveness can itself be a means of giving form to sections of a poem, without regard to the progress of an argument, a narrative, a descriptive

If the poet wished to reverse the tendency, he might crowd his expressive features into a few climactic lines and lighten the use of them in the others. For Pope such a solution was difficult. In too many of his works he tried to build the structure on general moral principles, and he tried to derive these principles from groups of concrete instances. Normally the instances lend themselves to expressive versification better than the inferences, since the latter, being more or less abstract, leave a poet little to copy through sound. As a result, the versification of the preliminary matter often distracts the reader from a would-be drum-rolling conclusion.

The *Essay on Man* repeatedly fails us in this way. We remember bits like the illustration of the five senses, with the balance of sharp and dull vowels in

> The mole's dim curtain, and the lynx's beam . . .
>
> [I.212]

or the subtle combination of pauses, sostenuto rhythm, and trailing alliteration in

> The spider's touch, how exquisitely fine!
> Feels at each thread, and lives along the line. . . .
>
> [I.217–18]

But who can state the hollow doctrine they lead to?[5] It is for such reasons that the *Essay on Man*, though hardly successful in any of its four epistles, grows weakest in the last. Concepts like happiness and humility must be embodied in particular, realized persons before they can challenge the true art of a poet like Pope. But for most of his fourth Epistle he treats them either abstractly or through fleeting allusions to individuals:

> To sigh for ribbands if thou art so silly,
> Mark how they grace Lord Umbra or Sir Billy:
> Is yellow dirt the passion of thy life?
> Look but on Gripus, or on Gripus' wife. . . .
>
> [IV.277–80]

There are not enough lines of character here for a poet to draw parallels in sound. The final paragraph, with its developed contrast between Bolingbroke and his dedicator, does supply a fair opportunity; and Pope rises to it in a celebrated image:

> Oh! while along the stream of Time thy name
> Expanded flies, and gathers all its fame,
> Say, shall my little bark attendant sail,
> Pursue the triumph, and partake the gale?

---

plan, or any other scheme derived from meaning. Those who find such a form to be a satisfactory literary structure will feel unmoved by my analyses.

[5] Recent expositions of the poem, I know, might contest my use of the epithet "hollow." None the less, I would adhere to it, supported by the view of Dr. Johnson and by many modern scholars and critics.

Thanks to the long vowels closed by *m* or *n*, the first of these couplets moves in a broad, sustained advance, while the *t*'s and short vowels of the second give it a lighter, quicker movement. Pope thus creates a delicate equivalent of the difference between the noble peer and the thin, small poet. Unfortunately, the plan of the *Essay* forced him to shift at the very end from this charming picture to a set of chilling maxims about social love and all that. The pull of the "little bark" therefore undermines the thumpery of those ultimate six lines, and instead of securing the climax he desired, the poet declines into an unintentional bathos.

For an even more radical disturbance of an intended structure by a triumph in the wrong part, the much-laboured *Epistle to Bathurst is* available. Reuben Brower has already suggested that the poet's heart was not in the apparent argument of this theodicy, and I agree.[6] Ironically, although the explicit declaration of positive doctrine is artfully placed and skilfully versified, its vapidity sinks it in comparison with what should be a less strirring paragraph. Certainly the character of the Man of Ross ought to dazzle the reader. To no section of the *Epistle* can we better apply Pope's often-quoted words about the whole, viz., "I never took more care in my life of any poem."[7]

We can trace the twenty couplets about Kyrle to a dramatic crest in the lines on his income.

> 'Oh say, what sums that gen'rous hand supply?
> What mines, to swell that boundless charity?'
> Of debts, and taxes, wife and children clear,
> This man possest—five hundred pounds a year.
> Blush, grandeur, blush! proud courts, withdraw your blaze!
> Ye little stars! hide your diminish'd rays.
>
> [ll. 251–90]

With "Blush, grandeur," and so on, the rhythm makes a bold shift obviously meant to convey the shock of the facts presented. Only three syllables in that lines are unstressed; the line is impeded by ponderous sounds and syntactic pauses. Add the prevalence of liquids and sibilants, and the modulation of vowels leading to the high note of "blaze"; then add the change from declarative statement to apostrophe. Together, such effects make a brilliant tonal contrast to the routine language and rhythm of the preceding lines. The rest of the couplet is less elaborate but still rich. On our way to these ingenuities we meet one instance after another of more subdued local expressiveness. The "Vaga" echoes; the Severn sounds hoarse; a "heav'n-directed spire" rises in a pyrrhic foot and a series of *i*'s. Even Kyrle's title of "Man of Ross" is converted to expressive purposes as babes lisp it in a sibilant line.

[6] *Alexander Pope: The Poetry of Allusion* (Oxford: Clarendon, 1959), pp. 257–60.

[7] Joseph Spence, *Anecdotes*, ed. S. Singer (London, 1820), p. 312.

Yet with all these precious elements Pope manufactured a disappointment. The character of Buckingham, in less than half the number of the lines on John Kyrle, has remained the poetic zenith of the third *Moral Essay*. To this degree the character of Buckingham has been ruinous to the rhetorical structure of the whole poem; it outshines both the positive moral ideal and the laborious tale of Sir Balaam, which concludes the work and ought to provide a sort of negative climax.

It would take a brave man to argue that the versification of the portrait of "great Villiers" surpassed that of Kyrle. In the later paragraph the turn comes with line 305, as Pope moves from Buckingham dying to the memory of the favorite's "life of pleasure." Before and after the change Pope's style is essentially the same: stichomythic, with strong caesuras, a profusion of monosyllables, and a steady beat of heavy iambics. The energy of the passage, the violence of the language, suggest the force of the speaker's emotion. In any local sense I find little expressiveness. Fascinating variety; magnificent suspense (from the periodic opening to the snowballing fragments of history recalled); an impulsive drive from the immediate present to a remote past, and then, by a quick process of detailed change, back to the present again. I find immense biographical appeal and ingenious rhetorical order, but not great expressiveness.

My deep appreciation of the devices I have been examining should be quite evident. If I find fault, it is in reaction against the often unqualified approval one meets of this aspect of Pope's genius. Surely a distinction has to be drawn between the finer and coarser forms his power took. That is, if we consider imitative or expressive versification even as such, with no regard to its impingement on the other elements of a poem, some kinds must deserve less praise than others.

There also remains a self-contradiction in the usual approach, in so far as it separates art from truth and encourages us to admire techniques without regard to the validity of the meaning supporting them. After all, expressiveness exists and can properly be judged solely in relation to the sense imitated by the sound. Purely musical variation or sonority, of the kind Samuel Say adored in *Paradise Lost*, may perhaps be independent of meaning—though I doubt it. But expressive versification has no other mode of life. The comparatively dry style of Wordsworth in the *Prelude* always operates as a magical counterpoint to the profundity of the experience he dealt with. The rich style of Pope failed when he tried to make it screen the shallowness of his argument.

With these principles in mind, I place the "echo to the sense" passage of the *Essay on Criticism* near the bottom of Pope's scale, not only for being coarse but also because the meaning of each illustration has no striking connection with its impact. Whether the alexandrine were a snake or a rope, whether Ajax or Sisyphus struggled with the rock, whether Camilla or Achilles skimmed along the main, would make no difference to the reader. Only when Timotheus comes on, and we approach Pope's praise of Dryden, does the choice of name or image grow cogent.

Windsor Forest, though an unsatisfactory whole,[8] has few things so obvious as this passage. When Pope describes the desolation left by William the Conqueror, he rises to a furious mingling of rage with description:

> The levell'd towns with weeds lie cover'd o'er,
> The hollow winds thro' naked temples roar;
> Round broken columns clasping ivy twin'd;
> O'er heaps of ruin stalk'd the stately hind;
> The fox obscene to gaping tombs retires,
> And savage howlings fill the sacred quires.
>
> [ll. 67–72]

Centered within a fifty-line paragraph, these couplets convey with apparent spontaneity both the poet's passion and the scene that provokes it. Thanks to their very regularity and weight, the accented vowels sound thunderously indignant. One may speculate that, the details being more appropriate to the sixteenth century than to the eleventh, Pope was able to sympathize with the victims of the Reformation more truly than with those of the Normans.[9] But whether or not this is so, it remains clear that the close of the passage, which should sound rich and triumphant, fails to come near the strength of these lines. I don't mean to rehearse my account of how local expressiveness can upset larger patterns; but judging the scene of desolation in itself, I have two comments to offer. First, we are drawn to interpret it as covertly anti-Reformation, because it does not fit even the vague impression we have of William I's reign. By treating the New Forest as if it were all England and by representing a few abandoned churches as if they were Christianity, Pope himself encourages us to look elsewhere. So the versification is too powerful for the ostensible subject. Second, if the description is to suggest ruin, it cannot be fortunate that the opulence of sound and rhythm connotes something grander and more interesting than the "teeming grain" and "ripen'd fields" with which the forest is contrasted. Instead of evoking a waste land, the versification hints at fulfillment.

Windsor Forest includes many such self-contradictions. The flight and death of the pheasant ought to sound pathetic, but they are far more en-

[8] Once again, I follow what might be called the orthodox judgment of men like Dr. Johnson and George Sherburn, although I appreciate the force of other accounts of the structure of the poem.

[9] Cf. note to line 68 of *Windsor Forest* in Pope, *Pastoral Poetry and An Essay on Criticism*, ed. E. Audra and Aubrey Williams (London: Methuen, 1961), p. 156.

grossing than the military episode just before them, and the reader's main feeling must be something like satisfaction. In the death of the larks a similar incongruity obtrudes itself, for the dazzling polish of the couplet extinguishes the pathos.

> Oft as the mounting larks their notes prepare,
> They fall, and leave their little lives in air.
>
> [ll. 133–34]

Charmed by the liquids, we ignore the creatures' fate. Because the poet renders the event only too well, he seems untrue to its meaning. When Lodona undergoes metamorphosis "in a soft, silver stream dissolv'd away," the flaw runs deeper; we not only miss the intended pathos but also return to the overexpressive manner of the *Essay on Criticism*.

I think we may generalize—or perhaps speculate—that a direct, unaffected private emotion is the hardest to convey through a locally expressive style. It is for "sincere" tenderness, spontaneous admiration, delivered as the inner feeling of the poet himself, that *ars celare artem* becomes essential. The less distance there must be between author and reader, the more "natural" the style should appear. In dramatic or deliberately mannered works, as in pastiche, the poet is removed far enough for obviously artful effects to be welcome; the same rule holds for passages of comedy and ridicule, where the poet is separating both the reader and himself from the subject of the poem.

So it seems natural that Pope's short pieces should rarely suffer from the faults I have been examining. Their brevity leaves small room for fragmentation and eliminates the collision of large and small patterns. Their subject is too narrow for many changes of tone; consequently, false tone becomes more avoidable. Many of Pope's short poems reveal a perfection that most of his long poems lack. All the more does one regret that academic criticism has laid so much weight on the big works.

In the *Epistle to Miss Blount with the Works of Voiture*—a short poem with an air of candor—we do not find much to call local expressiveness. Instead, there is an absolute sureness of touch from beginning to end. The poet wishes to sound graceful and melodious, but above all he must sound honest. Therefore, he works toward a subtle, general fitting of style to subject and mood. In a couplet like

> Ah quit not the free innocence of life
> For the dull glory of a virtuous wife!
>
> [ll. 45–46]

the impetus and irregularity of the rhythm delicately convey the unscreened movement of the speaker's sentiments. The couplets with no pause between lines have a parallel effect:

> Let the strict life of graver mortals be
> A long, exact, and serious comedy. . . .
>
> [ll. 21–22]

Throughout the poem the seesaw of false regulations and unconstrained virtue seems reflected by the fragile interplay of regular and irregular verse:

> Love, rais'd on beauty, will like that decay,
> Our hearts may bear its slender chain a day. . . .
>
> [ll. 63–64]

In this couplet the first line has two strong pauses, and only three of its syllables are clearly unaccented; it runs downhill toward "decay." The other line has a light, steady beat appropriate to "slender chain."

If I am right, we may surely trust Spence's report of Pope as saying, "There is scarce any work of mine in which the versification was more laboured than in my pastorals" (p. 312). The appeal of the *Pastorals* depends on our recognizing the conscious element of pastiche in their composition. We need not identify the allusions, but we must know that the poem is systematically conventional, that the poet was polishing themes, images, and phrases he received from a line of predecessors. Once we understand these primary facts, we can enjoy the brilliant versifying as a revelation of musical and expressive powers. Warton defined the principal merit of the *Pastorals* as "correct and musical versification; musical, to a degree of which rhyme could hardly be thought capable" (pp. 9–10). I think this judgment naturally suits a poem in which the author keeps himself at several carefully measured paces from the reader. The extraordinary evenness of surface in the *Pastorals*, the use of the same high finish and rich tones everywhere, seems correct for the same reasons. In these poems such essentials of design as narrative, persuasion, suspense, and climax hardly exist. The poet expects us to supply the thread of love intrigue; he provides the jeweled eulogies and sonorous laments. Significantly, Pope inscribed his favorite *Pastoral* to the memory of a woman he never knew.

> No grateful dews descend from ev'ning skies,
> Nor morning odours from the flow'rs arise.
> No rich perfumes refresh the fruitful field,
> Nor fragrant herbs their native incense yield.
>
> [*Autumn*, ll. 45–48]

A pack of lies, of course, but who cares? The almost uniform regularity of feet, broken by a single pyrrhic substitution, frames a lush variety of vowels and a stream of *f*'s with one or two *p*'s or *v*'s. Altogether, the sensuosities rejected by the meaning are amply affirmed by the versification, and the reader could hardly ask for more.

Pope's translations belong in a category near the *Pastorals*. In them, too, he could take the large structure for granted, as derived from famous models; and he also remained coolly separated from his own audience by the intervention of the original author. The expressive effects, whether local or general, are welcome because their ground is clear and fixed. But when Pope advanced to the imitations, a new and widely admired feat became normal. This is his free use of colloquial inflexions within the heroic couplet. So many critics have praised the accomplishment that I may only nod along with them. But even while agreeing that the range of Pope's work gains immensely from the incorporation of a true speaking voice, I have some observations. For one thing, apart from the *Epistle to Dr. Arbuthnot*, Pope's supreme masterpieces—like the *Rape of the Lock* and the second *Moral Essay*—make very restrained use of the inflections of common speech. For another, contrary to what is often implied, this was not something Pope had to learn late in his career. The *Epistle to Henry Cromwell*, written in 1707, is a brilliant example of the style. What happened is that Pope discovered how variously he could use it, especially as a starting point for modulating to the steepest height.

Using versification as a guide, I think we must conclude that Pope composed his greatest works when he invented a comprehensive structure that could hold—without contradictions or incongruities—the whole range of his expressive devices. The *Epistle to Dr. Arbuthnot* is such a poem; the *Rape of the Lock* is another; the second *Moral Essay* is a third. They have all received loving attention from the poet's admirers, and need no appreciation from me. In all of them Pope could shine freely without sacrificing climaxes to rival attractions. He could handle paragraphs as solid units and yet subordinate them to a larger action or rhetorical design. He could be his most artful while sounding spontaneous. When the Baron cuts Belinda's lock, Pope introduces a feminine rhyme to signalize the catastrophe and starts the second line of the couplet with a pyrrhic foot so that the gap will be obvious. But he also placed this supremely important action at the center of the poem; and because the mode of the work is sympathetic comedy, he profited from the humorous connotation of feminine rhymes. In the second *Moral Essay* the entrance of Mrs. Blount (l. 249) occasions a transformation of the meter from staccato violence, crackling with *p*'s, *t*'s, and strong pauses, to the sustained dignity of hardly broken lines drawn out with *m*'s, *b*'s, and open vowels. But this ingenious modulation, the most elaborate in the poem, also accompanies the main shift of interest—from the long examination of vicious women to the portrait of the virtuous Lady. Thus the intensity of the poet's feeling resides in the structure, versification, and meaning at once. Such poems cannot be overpraised.

Yet in judging versification, we can hardly expect all rational standards to be met at the same time (though many critics seem to assume this ought to happen). What wins by one measure may fail by another. We praise a poet for reconciling the syntax of speech to the demands of meter. We praise him again for using sound and rhythm expressively. We also praise him—or at least we used to—for fulfilling gracefully and musically the rules of an established pattern. Can a single style ignore none of these ideals? And yet more standards may flutter as the climate of taste changes. Saintsbury particularly commended Sackville's pleasing variations in phrase and pause; John Thompson sneers at such a "purely sonorous variety" and turns to praise Dolman for suiting his metrical pattern to his language and fulfilling a "dramatic intention."[10] If we accept this criterion, we judge versification by its appropriateness to the speaker of the lines. But if we follow Saintsbury, we judge by general rules of pleasing musicality, which are neither dramatic, nor locally expressive, nor closely related to the movement of natural speech.

My own opinion is that sheer musicality is now underestimated, and the relation between good verse and colloquial speech is exaggerated. To me, dramatic propriety seems only a minor feature of excellent versification—as it also is in prose so different as the Authorized Version of the Bible and the novels of Henry James. In the drama as such, different speakers may require different styles, and in any poem a shift from one speaker to another may be nicely evinced by rhythm and sound. But in nondramatic poetry the writer's tone, the general color of an episode or description, the dignity or triviality of a subject, should be overriding features. Beyond these lie the requirements of literary genre—the need, say, for a conventional love song to sound different from an epitaph. It is while holding such views that I have tried to examine the merits of Pope's versification.

It would be hard to overstate my admiration for Pope's genius. No other poet from the birth of Prior to the death of Cowper so fully repays the closest attention to his style. But I have tried to suggest that the enticements of local expressiveness could distract Pope from important structural demands, that the liveliness of his most expressive passages sometimes weakens the power of others that should sound more significant, and that for certain purposes a softening of his expressive powers might have been desirable.

If Pope himself is to blame for the term "correctness" as the mark of his literary achievement, we need not share that youthful opinion. But it is probably accurate to say that his failures, such as the "Man of Ross" passage, are ultimately failures of decorum. At least, I think we interpret both "correctness" and "decorum" most helpfully as appropriateness of

[10] *The Founding of English Metre* (London: Routledge and Kegan Paul, 1961), pp. 55, 56–61.

style; and if we employ this sense of the words, we can state Pope's fundamental problem as the discovery of subjects or arguments suited to his many styles. Versification then becomes not a good or bad thing in itself but the element of Pope's style that most subtly indicates when he is doing his finest work.

IV. The Cistern and the Fountain

Art and Reality in Pope and Gray

WHEN Edward Young found his satires "favourably received at home, and abroad," he supposed he could account for such good fortune by the remoteness of his derogatory observations—where they occurred—from specific human objects: "I am not conscious," he said (introducing an edition which was published the same year as *The Dunciad*), "of the least malevolence to any particular person thro' all the characters."[1] If Young sounds commonplace in recommending Horatian or "laughing" satire and condemning bitter, Juvenalian violence, he is equally representative of the critical truisms of his era in judging "general" satire to be a higher form than "particular." Like most satirists who flourished during the lives of Dryden and Swift, Young did of course enrich his generalities with a strong infusion of obvious particulars. Yet the structure and meaning of the seven poems never depend upon these changeable parts. In the final impression the reader's mind is occupied with permanent moral truths conveyed by vehicles or arguments that the concrete instances only decorate. The external realities surrounding the living poet are one order; the internal elements that constitute the poem are another.

In these prejudices Young curiously anticipated the widening practice of academic criticism during recent decades, or since the pedantries of philological and socio-historical research were rejected by young American scholars a generation ago. That the true structure of accepted masterpieces never depends upon their reference to nonliterary reality seems a natural law of learned criticism today. Ideally, it is an internal pattern that the "trained" reader hopes to find—a unifying design subtly harmonizing the superficially disparate images in a poem or connecting the various rhetorical figures with the character of a person supposed to speak the lines. To nourish the literary organism, one may indeed discover that profound intellectual traditions or ancient conventions of symbolism serve as reservoirs of allusions. But they in turn are self-contained imaginative or mythological reservoirs, distinct from factual history or from any science of observed human nature. If a would-be critic should now ask, in the style of Johnson, whether the argument of the *Essay on Man* is intellectually respectable,[2] whether it makes sense according to

[1] Preface to *Love of Fame, The Universal Passion* (London, 1728), sig. A2.

[2] In both the life of Pope and the review of Soame Jenyns.

nonpoetic logic or to principles of psychology, whether it agrees with our knowledge of the external, historical events of the period to which it was addressed, he would probably be censured for confusing literature with documentary evidence. The praise that Johnson devoted to Shakespeare's understanding of human behavior[3] finds only a low-keyed echo in the language of my colleagues. From the study of art and poetry alone, they often imply, we can learn what is most relevant to the appreciation of literary structures, although the accidents of a poem may receive helpful clarification from ancillary knowledge.

In the study of eighteenth-century literature this view has gained coincidental strength from the widely accepted belief that impersonal art is the hallmark of Augustan craftsmanship. The final pages of *Gulliver's Travels*, in which Swift spoke out loud and clear, we are commonly asked to regard as peripheral to the main design. Poems like Johnson's elegy on Levet are passed under our inspection to demonstrate that even the private crises of an author were characteristically generalized and purified before a truly Augustan artist employed them in a work for publication. As an attribute enhancing the ideal of a self-contained literary structure, the value of impersonality is evident.

I am inclined to question the usefulness of these postulates, not with any hope of destroying them but rather in an effort to define the range of their effectiveness. Nobody would like to see us return to that Mesozoic era when the biography of an author was indistinguishable from the criticism of his work, or to that later but glacial age when the history of the language or the social development of the nation was presumed to cast the ultimate illumination upon both the import and the importance of a poem. Yet if internal "literary" coherence has been established, unconsciously, as the highest principles that a scholarly critic can demonstrate in a classic he admires, perhaps it would be profitable to examine some consequences of that assumption. My own hesitant, exploratory effort can hardly generate a conclusive proof or disproof, for my argument is not the sort that knocks down one general proposition and sets up a replacement. Rather I hope by using suggestive examples to encourage others to test my case with evidence of their own picking. In this effort I shall take up a few masterpieces and failures of eighteenth-century poetry, inquiring whether the structural integrity of each does not depend for its cogency, or deepest appeal, upon allusions to reality—whether, in other words, the truly successful imaginative structures do not reach out like a fountain whose glittering shape overflows into and thus vivifies the world around it. Among the specimens to be examined here, two, Pope's *Epistle to a Lady* and Gray's *The Bard*, enjoy a rich-

[3] Particularly in the Preface to the edition of Shakespeare.

ness of self-contained form that has, I think, seldom been adequately appreciated.

Few of Pope's works pretend to exhibit throughout the sort of design which his couplets and his verse paragraphs possess. I wish now to argue that the second *Moral Essay, An Epistle to a Lady, Of the Characters of Women,* has just this virtue in addition to its others.[4] *To a Lady* is a finished masterpiece such as Pope rarely created. Parts of it have received praise from William Empson and Lytton Strachey.[5] Yet little attention has fallen, I think, on the elaborated form of the whole poem. So I should like to consider this in terms of the arrangement of parts and pattern of images, and then to ask how it depends on allusions to reality. Through comparisons with similar poems by both Pope and Edward Young, I hope to show that the achievement is remarkable.

The *Epistle to a Lady* can be divided into three parts: the first two hundred lines are a group of portraits of women, mostly sinners; the next fifty lines are a didactic analysis of their sins; and the final forty lines are a eulogy addressed to a Lady listener, easily identifiable as Martha Blount. Portraits, analysis, eulogy—among these the connection seems obvious. The concentrated praise in lines 249 to 292 balances the distributed attacks in lines 1 to 198, and the analysis in lines 199 to 248 forms a bridge between the two. The virtues the Lady owns—modesty, tenderness, fidelity—are conspicuously those the sinners lack; and their vices—vanity, avarice, ambition, lust—have no place in her character.

The structure of the first section will easily be seen to have a formal order. Thus in the series of portraits we find several kinds of rising lines. For one thing, the poet surveys his sinners roughly in order of size: a couplet or two on each of the first few names; four couplets on Silia; six on Calypso; eight on Narcissa; nine on Philomede; seven on Flavia; eighteen on Atossa; and twelve on Cloe, with some very brief profiles interspersed. In the *Epistle to Bathurst,* Pope had used the same rough order of size: one couplet on Colepepper, eight on Blunt, twenty-two on Sir Balaam, and so forth; the principle seems ordinary enough. But in the *Epistle to a Lady* Pope combined it with another, which Elder Olson has noticed in the *Epistle to Dr. Arbuthnot.*[6] There, as the speech progresses, the satire sharpens: the portrait of Atticus is more severe than the ridicule of fools at the beginning, and the portrait of Sporus is more severe than that of Atticus. So in the *Epistle to a Lady,* Atossa's portrait is the climax

4 Cf. Frank Brady, "The History and Structure of Pope's 'To a Lady,'" *SEL,* 9 (1969), 439–62, for evidence of Pope's changes of plan in the long history of the composition of the poem.

5 Empson, *Seven Types of Ambiguity* (London: Chatto and Windus, 1930), pp. 161–62; Strachey, *Pope* (New York: Harcourt, Brace, 1926), pp. 30–31.

6 "Rhetoric and the Appreciation of Pope," *MP,* 37 (1939), 13–35.

of violence as well as the climax in length; Philomede's is milder; Narcissa's, still milder. But, as it happens, the sinners are also arranged in degrees of reality. Out of the first six, five seem fictitious; i.e., the poem does not invite us to search for an original. But Sappho, the next, can only refer to Lady Mary Wortley Montagu. Four additional pseudonyms—Philomede, Flavia, Atossa, and Cloe—have been associated with the second Duchess of Marlborough, the Duchess of Montagu, the Duchess of Buckinghamshire, and the Countess of Suffolk. Finally, the queen is actually named, as is the Duchess of Queensberry (who does not, however, count as a sinner).[7] From the pseudonymous and fictitious, therefore, through the pseudonymous but recognizable, Pope moves to proper public names; and from a countess and an earl's daughter, through duchesses, he rises to the queen. Admitting many irregularities and interruptions, we may say that he moves roughly through degrees of reality and degrees of rank. In other words, as Pope gets further along in the poem and strengthens his grip on the audience, he grows bolder.

There is a further meaning to Pope's order. Those women who can be identified are peeresses or royalty, in contrast to the humble station of Mrs. Blount. Such targets of course give weight to the poem, just as an imperial dramatis personae gives weight to tragedy. They are courtiers, natural focuses of national concern. Lady Irwin had remarked of the *Epistle to Bathurst*, "As the objects of [Pope's] satire are low, people will be less offended, for who cares for [Peter] Waters, Charters, or Ward."[8] One never feels that the figures of *An Epistle to a Lady* are too inconsequential to be worth reading about. As we approach the peak of society, however, we approach the peak of corruption; the poet evokes an urgency suggesting a national crisis.

Young had two satires on women that deeply influenced Pope's work—numbers five and six of *The Universal Passion*, which are commonly judged to be the most satisfactory poems in that book. Yet Young completely missed Pope's effect of urgency because not only did he assign no particular ranks to his group of criminals but he also singled out royalty as the example of virtue:

> 'Midst empire's charms, how *Carolina's* heart
> Glows with the love of *virtue, and of art*?
>
> [Satire VI, p. 155]

But Pope, from the long sequence of portraits, swings us up through the passage of didactic analysis into the final eulogy of Mrs. Blount, and

[7] For these identifications, see F. W. Bateson's edition of Pope's *Epistles to Several Persons*, Twickenham edition of the *Poems of Alexander Pope*, III, Pt. ii, 2nd ed. (London: Methuen, 1961), pp. xxxv–xlviii.

[8] Letter of January 18, 1733/4, in Historical Manuscript Commission, *XV Report*, Appendix, Pt. VI, p. 97.

there he shifts his point of view, for he addresses the poem to the good woman and holds up the vicious to her examination. Their corrupted natures are described in the third person; her virtuous self, in the second. They are spoken about; she is present, to be saluted directly. The effect gives to goodness, in its limited space, an immediacy and a substance which evil, though intensely realized and extended over hundreds of lines, has lacked. On this drawn-out moral contrast the poem is built. Like the coils of a long spring, the vicious characters are stretched at length and then let go to provide rebounding impetus for the final panegyric.

The moral implications of this relationship bear out the formal order. The Lady is both the positive climax of the entire poem and the justification of the satire. Obviously, Pope wished to compliment Martha Blount. But in an age when sincerity was the most imitative form of flattery, and in a poem which singled out panegyric as the most suspect kind of literature, he had to exert himself to give force to his praise. By employing most of his lines in condemnation of dangerous women, he adds distinction to the solitary approval bestowed upon Mrs. Blount. Conversely, by loudly recognizing virtue as it appears in a unique specimen, he gives energy to his dispraise of vice. Years earlier, in the *Epistle to Burlington*, Pope had followed the same method; but there the attack on Timon is so much longer than the neighboring eulogy of Burlington, and so far more brilliant, that it submerges the latter. In both cases, however, Pope is especially convincing because as a normal thing he places an envoi or apostrophe, addressed to a primary reader, at the end of a long poem. Since this person is conventionally given his proper name, as the subject of a public tribute, the anonymous Lady inherits such authenticity. Here Pope is in a sense merely expanding and heightening the envoi so that it becomes the positive climax of his poem.

The apotheosis of Mrs. Blount also helps Pope meet a demand normally attached to the production of satire. By what right, a reader naturally wonders, does any author take it upon himself to expose so many faults in others? Most satirists answer by making explicit their moral principles and thereby establishing their own integrity. Thus in *An Epistle to Dr. Arbuthnot*, Pope displayed the poet himself as *integer vitae scelerisque purus*, to balance the ignobility of his enemies. This makes sense rhetorically, but the inevitable suggestion of vanity weakens his power as a satirist. In the *Epistle to a Lady* he works less directly but places himself more effectively under the banner of righteousness, for here he embodies virtue in another person and then aligns himself with her. To incarnate his positive values, he invokes not a set of propositions but the concrete description of Martha Blount. Where he does have a long generalizing, didactic passage—and that is to bridge the great series of vicious women and the final portrait of his heroine—he is not expounding virtue but analyzing evil. By establishing his friend as his standard, Pope not only makes his ideal vivid; he also gives us implicit assurance of his own moral elevation. Since she appears as goodness itself, and he makes himself out to be her wholesale and accepted admirer, Mrs. Blount has the effect of a supreme character witness for him, and thereby encourages us to accept his denunciation of the world. Although Pope had employed a similar method at the close of the *Epistle to Burlington*, the tie between the earl and the poet is too thin, and the effect correspondingly weak.

If the formal order of parts thus reveals extraordinary internal coherence directed to a significant rhetorical purpose, the pattern of imagery in the *Epistle* supplies some fascinating reinforcement of that impression. We must remember that *To a Lady* presents a dramatic situation in which the readers overhear the poet as he talks to a woman friend about some paintings. The pair are strolling through a gallery or around a studio hung with portraits and sketches of ladies. As they stop before the various pictures or studies, the poet delivers remarks on the subjects. At the end of the tour and the end of the poem, he turns to his friend and pronounces an encomium contrasting her with the persons whose character he has just unmasked.

It was a traditional literary device, as Jean Hagstrum has shown, to use a gallery of painted portraits as the imagined scene of a disquisition upon moral types.[9] Pierre Lemoyne had employed it in his *Peintures Morales* (1645). Farquhar staged the idea in the *Beaux' Stratagem*, and Addison supplied an instance in a *Spectator* paper (no. 83). Professor Hagstrum also reminds us of the convention of satire formulated as instructions given to a painter. This was established by the Italian, Busenello, in his serious panegyric, *Il Trionfo Veneziano*, where the poet does not describe scenes directly but tells an artist how to represent them. Waller, one of Pope's acknowledged masters, naturalized the device to England when he composed a eulogy upon the Duke of York's heroism during a naval battle; here again the poet tells an artist how to bring out the value of the scenes, and Waller entitled his work *Instructions to a Painter*. The formula was soon copied by satirists as a means of pinpointing the corruptions of Charles II's court. Although most of these bitter, libelous pieces seem ephemeral, at least two are by Andrew Marvell.[10] Pope is only

[9] For my discussion of the metaphors drawn from painting I am indebted to Hagstrum's *The Sister Arts: The Tradition of Literary Pictorialism and English Poetry from Dryden to Gray* (Univ. of Chicago Press, 1958), pp. 236–40, and to Robert J. Allen's "Pope and the Sister Arts" in *Pope and His Contemporaries: Essays Presented to George Sherburn*, ed. James L. Clifford and Louis A. Landa (Oxford: Clarendon, 1949), pp. 78–88.

[10] See H. M. Margoliouth's discussion in his edition of Marvell's *Poems and Letters* (Oxford: Clarendon, 1927), I, 268–70, 289.

tangentially instructing a painter, and his scheme is far more peripheral than either Waller's or Marvell's. However, the tradition was familiar to him; and for the reader who remembers the Restoration poems, the overtone is there:

> Chuse a firm cloud, before it fall, and in it
> Catch, ere she change, the Cynthia of this minute.
>
> . . . . .
>
> Some wand'ring touches, some reflected light,
> Some flying stroke alone can hit 'em right.
>
> [ll. 19–20, 153–54]

All this is figurative, of course; for we normally treat the Lady of the poem as a transparent screen between the poet and ourselves; we treat the poem as a monologue; and we treat the allusions to painting as metaphors. However, I should like to indicate what the figurative setting contributes to the design and rhetoric of the poem. Young, like Pope, stated his theme in terms of painting, and he made casual use of plastic similes:

> What picture's yonder loosen'd from its frame?
> Or is't Asturia? that affected dame?
>
> [Satire VI, p. 144]

But he never hinted at more or connected the separate similes to a general scheme. Pope, however, explores the symbolic value of treating sinners this way; and he puts his meaning explicitly at the opening of the attack. In his substitution of paintings for persons he implies the vices of vanity, deceit, and—above all—fickleness:

> How many pictures of one nymph we view,
> All how unlike each other, all how true!
>
> [ll. 5–6]

Pope contrasts the corrupted women's dependence upon visible charms with the Lady's reliance on virtue within. The theme is a commonplace: Juba's praise of Marcia in *Cato*, Swift's praise of Biddy Floyd, Welsted's epilogue to Steele's *Conscious Lovers*, all sing the same tune, exalting not the visible but the moral, intellectual, and domestic resources of the ideal woman; yet in Pope's poem the implicit contrast, point for point, with the tangibilities of the villainous women who have just been observed, produces a marvelous ironical transformation of the adjectives associated with them—"art," "pride," and so on—when these are applied to Mrs. Blount:

> Reserve with frankness, art with truth ally'd,
> Courage with softness, modesty with pride,
> Fix'd principles, with fancy ever new.
>
> [ll. 277–79]

Young published similar aphorisms: "Your strongest charms are native innocence"; "Be kind and virtuous, you'll be blest and wise." But he confused his arguments by also praising good women for appearances—for physical beauty and elegant clothes; he never tied the moral contrast to a pervasive metaphor; and his flattery of the highest-born compelled him to shun opportunities for irony.

While Pope's objects of satire are present only as paintings, his Lady appears as a living being. The two-dimensional portraits therefore enhance one's sense of positive climax, because it is only after passing over these dozen surfaces that we meet the rounded heroine. To Pope's remark that we distinguish such females by their color—"black, brown, or fair"—Professor Hagstrum applies the principle, accepted by Pope's generation of connoisseurs, that line is more real and stable than color, that color is more changeable and therefore like women (pp. 236–40). The same motif occurs in the *Essay on Criticism*, where the "faithful pencil" is opposed to "treacherous colours," and where the true lines of sound judgment are contrasted with the deceitful colors of false learning:

> But as the slightest sketch, if justly trac'd,
> Is by ill *colouring* but the more disgrac'd,
> So by *false learning is good sense* defac'd.
>
> [ll. 23–25]

The motif appears again in the lines on Cynthia in the *Epistle to a Lady*:

> Come then, the colours and the ground prepare!
> Dip in the rainbow, trick her off in air.
>
> [ll. 17–18]

And later in the poem it is employed more generally:

> Pictures like these, dear Madam, to design,
> Asks no firm hand, and no unerring line.
>
> [ll. 151–52]

Pope even suggests that simple or unmixed (i.e., "equal") colors will not suit the problem, for only blended paints, implicitly less pure than the unmixed, can represent woman's evanescence and superficiality:

> For how should equal colours do the knack?
> Chameleons who can paint in white and black?
>
> [ll. 155–56]

Within the paintings Pope made further refinements. The pseudonymous women pose generally in costume or disguise, and not as themselves; and the costume is often of a mythological rather than historical figure: false names, false dress, false models. Or the sinners pose ironically as saints—Mary Magdalen, Cecilia. To such tokens of deception is linked the ancient contrast between naked truth and overdressed vice.

> Artists! who can paint or write,
> To draw the naked is your true delight.
> That robe of quality so struts and swells,
> None see what parts of nature it conceals.
>
> [ll. 187–90]

Professor Hagstrum reminds us of Titian's *Sacred and Profane Love*, in which sacred love is naked and profane love clothed (pp. 236–40). It is also obviously symbolic that the same woman should adopt contradictory roles in different paintings. The very syntax of such descriptions presses ambiguity upon us:

> Arcadia's Countess, here, in ermin'd pride,
> Is there, Pastora by a fountain side.
>
> [ll. 7–8]

The couplet seems deliberately paradoxical. Although she comes from Arcadia and should therefore be a shepherdess, she poses for one picture in the robes of a peeress; on the contrary, although her husband is presumably Earl of Pembroke and a great courtier, she disguises herself in the pendant picture as a country lass.

Finally, the metaphor of painting is borne out in the use of color imagery to contrast the Lady and the sinners. Gray and silver belong to her; red and gold to them; her scene is shaded; theirs is dazzling; she evokes the quiet moon, they the beaming sun. Since the Lady happens to be a spinister, the lunar tones appropriately suggest Diana and chastity.

If one were simply adhering to the principle of self-contained art, this point might well be the stopping place of criticism. The internal structure of Pope's poem has been, however hastily (I have not even mentioned the brilliant versification of the couplets leading up to the introduction of Mrs. Blount) set forth; his superiority to a rival (and mentor) has been indicated. Yet the power of the *Epistle* is obviously too great for one to feel right about leaving it so soon; the poem overflows, reaching beyond literature into reality. It is in the very structure of the *Epistle* that the overflowing occurs most beautifully, but the effect is evident as well in humbler ways that may be noticed first. There is, for example, a historical truth in the imagined situation. Pope had early experience of pictures like those he described; he took painting lessons from Jervas; he was accustomed to thinking of poetry in pictorial terms; and he was accustomed to hearing an artist discuss painting in literary terms.[11] Though for him

[11] On Pope's interest in painting and his connection with Jervas, see George Sherburn, *The Early Career of Alexander Pope* (Oxford, 1934), esp. pp. 69 and 102–3. For the correspondence between Jervas and Pope, see the first volume of Sherburn's edition of Pope's *Correspondence* (Oxford, 1956), esp. pp. 189, 239, 315, 332.

pictorial art was divided, in the curious categories of his age, between portraits and history painting, it was of portraits that he had the most experience; all his own efforts were in that category. He had, as it happens, seen pictures of some of the women to whom he alludes in the poem; he had himself copied one—the Duchess of Montagu—on canvas; and he had commissioned and owned at least two—Mrs. Blount herself and Lady Mary.[12] Since Mrs. Blount spent much time in his house, therefore, the setting of the poem is remarkably close to reality. Of course, Pope shielded himself by the use of misleading details. To smother rumors and to protect the maiden Lady of his poem, he gave her a husband and a daughter; yet we all know she was drawn from the spinster Martha Blount.

As it was originally printed, the poem suffered enormous excisions, the most sensational characters being prudently omitted until Pope felt secure enough to face the consequences of releasing them—or else so near death that no consequence could touch him.[13] He would hardly have held back from publication the magnificent lines on Philomede, Atossa, Cloe, and Caroline if they were not allusions to the second Duchess of Marlborough, the Duchess of Buckinghamshire, the Countess of Suffolk, and the queen. Sappho has been universally taken as a lampoon on Lady Mary Wortley Montagu. Arcadia's Countess is probably Margaret, first wife of the eighth earl of Pembroke. This employment of recognizable people and events is one persuasive ground of Pope's satirical appeal. Poetically he keeps hinting, "These things have really happened." He does not mean that every name alludes to an existing person or that every rumored scandal is true as represented. But since he claims that his insights are worth our attention, he must assume the wisdom of experience. By implying that he has observed at first hand the profusion of cases displayed in his argument, he encourages the reader to take him seriously. As a corollary, if the reader is to trust the obvious fables, he must recognize some facts. Just as Pope's didactic propositions shade from overt conventionalities to covert audacities, so his factual allusions shade from parables to direct reporting. The truisms serve to win the reader's faith so that he will respect the individual judgments; the facts season the legends so that the reader may credit the author as both an experienced and a faithful historian.

A more special effect is also felt because one never can be certain whether the poet created an example or witnessed it. Once the reader thinks he can correctly name a pseudonymous character, he is bound to keep searching for new clues; and this search adds to Pope's late satires a

[12] See Bateson's note to *Moral Essay* I.107; Pope's *Correspondence*, I, 189, and II, 21–22; and Pope's *Minor Poems*, Twickenham ed., VI, ed. N. Ault and J. Butt (London: Methuen, 1954), pp. 211–12.

[13] Bateson, ed., *Epistles to Several Persons*, pp. ix–xvi, 40–44.

vibrancy which deepens and strengthens their rhetoric. Young, in his satires, both sacrificed this special effect and weakened his general argument by dropping clues to a subject's name only when he was praising the person. His topical allusions are, as a careful scholar remarks, "not malicious," and individuals, if pointed out at all, are "generally mentioned in flattering terms."[14] Our curiosity is therefore dampened rather than aroused, and we infer that evil has less power than good.

The most brilliant allusion to reality, and the last effect I shall analyze in the poem, is central to the structure. This occurs at the negative climax and peripety, as Pope is completing and abandoning his collection of sinners; and it shows how a rhetorical order can be determined by facts external to a literary work. With the sequence of Atossa, Cloe, the queen, and the Duchess of Queensberry, Pope seems to have plotted his path so as to reveal the sharpest contrast between the vicious and the good. He almost certainly intended the Duchess of Buckinghamshire to be recognized in Atossa. Katherine Darnley, Duchess of Buckinghamshire and Normanby, was the illegitimate daughter of James II. All her life, she exhibited a paranoid pride in her ancestry; she had a long feud with her husband's bastards, became famous for her megalomania, and ended up insane by any definition. "Cloe" almost certainly points to Henrietta Howard, Countess of Suffolk. She was at the same time both lady-in-waiting to the queen and *maîtresse en titre* to the king. But although, as Prince of Wales, he had indeed made love to her, she was now superannuated, overweight, and deaf. It was years since he had shown her much tenderness. At court she endured the contemptuous protection of the queen, who did not wish her to be replaced by a less manageable instrument. The Countess of Suffolk was Pope's neighbor and friend.

Of course, the lines on Caroline are cautious. Pope discusses neither the queen nor a painting of her. Instead, he ridicules the stereotype that always seems to be substituted for a description when a painter or author must represent the majesty of Britain. There is a parallel passage in Pope's version of Horace's *Satires*, II.i, addressed to Fortescue (ll. 21–32). No scholar seems to have observed that in both places the poet was probably alluding to Young's tinny tributes, in his satires, to the queen and her eldest daughter.[15] It is such cliché praises and cliché poses that Pope pretends to be attacking, rather than the royal person. Because of these screens of nonsense, he says, one cannot look to the throne for a model of virtue.

[14] Charlotte E. Crawford, "What Was Pope's Debt to Edward Young?" *ELH*, 13 (1946), 161.

[15] Young, *Universal Passion*, satire V, p. 113; satire VI, pp. 155–56. Cf. Crawford, p. 167. The ridicule of the stereotype-maker is also found in the *Epistle to Cobham*, II. 87–92. The end of *To Augustus* is, I suppose, the last refinement of the theme.

As an alternative, however, he suggests, of all people, an avowed enemy of the court, whose title has a pun on "queen." Catherine Douglas, Duchess of Queensberry, was celebrated not only for her beauty and wit. She had bestowed the most liberal patronage on Pope's friend, Gay; and recently she had withdrawn from court because of a furious quarrel with the royal household over her grace's aggressive support of Gay's opera *Polly*. Nevertheless, says Pope, this duchess is too modest to act as a cynosure. He will therefore pass on to the general fact that humble persons are easier to see truly than the great; and the humble, therefore, will better provide us with examples. "If Queensberry to strip there's no compelling / 'Tis from a handmaid we must take a Helen" (ll. 193–94).

In giving us a king's bastard, followed by a king's mistress, followed by the same king's queen, to whom the same mistress was lady-in-waiting, followed by a Duchess of Queensberry who had thrown over the whole court, I think Pope must have been sounding a fanfare of innuendoes to draw attention to his theme and to announce his heroine.[16] Yet it is only by going outside the poem, to external facts, that we can establish the meaning of this sequence. We have touched the point of the social pyramid and found it the pinnacle of evil as well as of rank: the greatest vanity, the greatest lust, and the greatest power appear together; and since it is here alone that Pope used proper names, we may also say this marks his most direct appeal to reality.[17]

Applying to Young the test that Pope meets so easily, one produces quite different results; for at several points Young may be described as defeated by reality. As a comprehensive principle the argument to which he tried to relate all the instances of vice or frivolity in his satires seems unpleasantly shallow; namely, that a desire for fame of one sort or another is the common source of foolish and vicious actions. Young may perhaps have flattered himself that he had a proposition to prove—and consequently more intellectual coherence than Pope in the *Epistle*—but the proposition is so weak and unconvincing as to disgrace its asserter. Even if it should be regarded not as a supposed truth but merely as a structural device, it fails, because many of the most effective passages in the poems cannot be related to the central theme—the denunciation of patron-hunters:

> Who'd be a *crutch* to prop a rotten peer;
> Or living *pendant*, dangling at his ear.
>
> [Satire IV, p. 71]

[16] The reference in l. 198 to "honest Mah'met," a servant to George II, seems intended to strengthen the innuendoes.

[17] Cf. Bateson's comment, p. xlviii, on the accuracy of the poem. Pope's allusions to Martha Blount in his letters and the contrast he draws between her and Lady Suffolk are remarkably close to his language in the poem; see his *Correspondence*, III, 349, 434–35, 450, and IV, 187.

The failure of the poems to cohere as a general argument would seem less offensive if Young allowed subordinate pleadings to move consistently with themselves. But repeatedly when he claims to fight for one doctrine, he wears the uniform of another. In his own person, for example, he reproaches venal authors and bemoans the willingness of poets to sacrifice truth to profit. Yet in the dedications, compliments, and apostrophes that intermit the satire, his quivering eagerness for mercenary advancement appears so openly that no reader can observe the reproaches without sneering. Furthermore, the portraits that seem to excite the poet's greatest energy do not exhibit threats to a real order of morality but reveal mere freaks or triflers, such as Brabantio, who is proud of a reputation for absentmindedness (satire III, p. 49). Normally, one has little sense that the characters are drawn from living people; they are too often governed by meaningless whimsies, and Young too willingly abandons the facts of human nature to satisfy his love of paradox—as in the character of Philander, who secretly loves his own charming wife but publicly keeps a mistress to avoid an unfashionable reputation (satire III, pp. 54–55). Young's supreme blunder, in a work supposed to advance virtue and ridicule vice, was to choose his objects of admiration from the irregular circles of political power. Several of his eulogies would, with no other change, become ironical insults if set in the frame of some lines by Pope. The fawning praise of Dodington (whom sober historians compare to a jackal, the exaltation of a pawn like Compton—"the *crown*'s asserter, and the *people*'s friend"! (satire IV, p. 63)—imply a contempt for the reality of British public life that vitiates Young's attack upon corrupt politicians (satire III, pp. 56–60). As a final and wholly appropriate streamer to trail after his wobbling car, Young consecrated his closing "satire" to the climactic and wildly indecorous flattery of Walpole and the king.

The two satires (V and VI) that Young allotted to women rise to a far higher level of art than the rest of the *Universal Passion*, but no judge has yet accused Young of an excess of craftsmanship in these poems. Probably the most brilliant piece of poetry between the works of Pope and the works of Blake is Gray's *The Bard*, against whose splendor the accusation might easily be brought. Once more, however, I think the astonishing internal, literary coherence of the poem has been insufficiently appreciated, and again I think the test of reality can bring out aspects of the poem that are fundamental to its value. The essential design of *The Bard* has a deep similarity to that of Pope's *Epistle*; for if we mark line 101 (two-thirds of the way through) as the turning point, the ode comprises a long first part, aggressive and denunciatory, which is balanced by a shorter second part, affirmative and confident. Within this general contrast Gray, like Pope, established a set of symmetrical parallels. Thus the poem both opens and closes with a confrontation between Edward I and the last of the Welsh bards, on Mount Snowdon, with the Conway River running below. After cursing the king, the bard bemoans the deaths of his fellow poets and then foretells the miseries of Edward's descendants as far as Richard III. At the peripety, the predictions of doom are symmetrically transformed into a paean of joy as the bard envisions the triumph of Welsh blood in the Tudor dynasty. This is symmetrically followed by a celebration of the Elizabethan literary renaissance, to match the lament over the singers murdered by Edward. Finally, in a gesture that reverses his opening challenge when he looked down from a beetling rock upon the descending army of invaders, the bard leaps triumphantly to his suicide in the "roaring tide" of the river.

In its general movement the poem opposes impetuosity to formal restraint. There is a boldness or extravagance in the action, imagery, and language which is met by a fixed complexity in the versification. The mountain landscape is deliberately sublime, anticipating the climactic scene of *The Prelude*.[18] Gushing under the peak, the river bears connotations suggestive of the creative flow of the poetic imagination as detailed in *The Progress of Poesy*. The bard poses in a style which recalls Raphael's representation of God appearing to Ezekiel, as Gray himself noted. It is therefore as an embodiment of the divinely creative principle that the bard stands higher than the king and the royal army. To intensify the terror that sublimity requires, Gray does not entrust the prophetic verses merely to the bard but rather gives them to a chorus of spirits—ghosts of the slaughtered poets—who are seen and heard by their living confrere. At the turning point, they complete their prophecy and vanish, to be replaced by the revelation to the bard of a visionary pageant that displays Tudor monarchs, courtiers and poets, with Milton bringing up the rear.

Gray's boldly inventive vocabulary, his sudden shifts of point of view, the sensational choice of historical detail (including royal murders, civil wars, and infanticide), all strengthen the rushing violence that marks the poem. By exaggerating his normally rich use of expressive sound effects, Gray adds to the impetuosity of the movement. There is a quasi-onomatopoeia in a line like, "He wound with toilsome march his long array" (l. 12) or "Regardless of the sweeping whirlwind's sway" (l. 75). But the elaborate use of alliteration assonance, chiasmus, internal rhyme, and similar devices seems dramatically appropriate as well, because Welsh poetry is characterized by such intricacies; notice, for example, the

[18] Though Gray's influence on Wordsworth hardly wants demonstration—particularly in connection with his taste for mountains—I should like to call attention to the note, in the Selincourt-Darbishire ed. of *The Prelude* (Oxford: Clarendon, 1959), on V, 581–601 of the 1805 text.

expressive contrast, before and after the caesura in line 71, of the same fricatives, sibilants, and liquids: "Fair laughs the morn, and soft the zephyr blows." On a modern ear the boldness of Gray's diction is dulled by the freedom that recent generations have exercised in altering old meanings and creating neologisms. Yet expressions like "lyon-port," "crested pride," and "hoary hair / Stream'd, like a meteor, to the troubled air" (ll. 117, 9, 19–20) still retain some of the shocking power that disgusted Johnson in spite of Gray's care to model his adjectival nouns and remote analogies upon authoritative example.

As a countervortex to the bursting richness of action, scene, and style, Gray imposed upon these elements the steady impulse of his formidable metrics and rhyme scheme. By refining on the form of the "true" Pindaric ode, he arrived at a triple-ternary structure, the whole work comprising three main units, each of which in turn contains three stanzas: a paired strophe and antistrophe and an epode. To tighten the already tight form, Gray required not only that each antistrophe match its own strophe (an elaborate stanza form of his own invention), foot for foot and rhyme for rhyme, but also that precisely the same form be employed for all three pairs. Similarly, all three epodes possess a common, even more complicated stanzaic pattern. In order to clarify for the ear this articulated structure, Gray ends each stanza with an alexandrine preceded by a rhyming pentameter. To give a sense of burgeoning progression, he concentrates the short verses at the beginning of the stanza and makes the line lengths expand near the end; thus each strophe and antistrophe opens with five tetrameter verses and closes with five pentameters before the alexandrine. Combining brevity with abruptness to give the effect of a sudden start ("Ruin seize thee, ruthless King!"), Gray omits the first syllable of the first line of each strophe and antistrophe, so that it sounds trochaic and is shorter than any other line except the fifth, which is heptasyllabic as well (I suppose to regularize the effect). In the epodes each stanza begins with trimeters, has a heptasyllabic eighth line, and uses internal rhyme in the fifteenth and seventeenth lines (enriching the cadence of approaching conclusion). Although the stanzas are long, Gray breaks them up into distinct quatrains, sestets, and couplets. The strophes and antistrophes work out curiously like a Shakespearean sonnet; the epodes are composed of a sestet at either end, joined by two quatrains.

This whole, charted, subdivided apparatus of verses and rhymes is worked in counterpoint with the narrative of the poem. As in Pindar, the meaning often ignores the breaks between stanzas, and the pauses or transitions often occur at odd points within a stanza. The reader cannot help feeling the dancelike interplay of meaning and form, boldness and restraint, motion and fixity.

In spite of its manifest brilliance *The Bard* is widely acknowledged to be a failure. Why? I think the essential reason will be found in the weakness of the poem's appeal to reality. Unlike Pope, Gray, so far from inviting such a test, utterly evades it. This evasion appears in the very structure of the story. Indubitably, the poet asks us to treat the incident as fantasy. For all the vividness of the representation, for all the fullness of historical reference, the episode has no claim to authenticity. The text is largely devoted to the speech of the bard. Yet this speaker kills himself as soon as his monologue is over and cannot, therefore, transmit his account to any reporter. On the English side no one is supposed to understand Welsh; and if anyone did, the details of events that have not yet occurred and that are forecast with an obscurity hiding their meaning even from the bard would be unintelligible. That Edward killed the Welsh singers might be known; what one of those singers prophesied alone, just before his death, and to an uncomprehending audience could not possibly be preserved. The intellectual implications of the poem also remain as unreal today as they appear in Johnson's critique of *The Progress of Poesy.*[19] Contrary to Gray's argument, the true poet is not always patriotic; he does not necessarily defend freedom; if he lives in a "primitive" rural society, he will not write more "sublime" songs than a cultivated, urban poet (Milton and Caradoc make strange yokemates to draw Gray's "presumptuous car"); and finally, genius does not tend to flourish under a good government or to wither under despotism.

On the other hand, Gray's most successful poem has a positive bearing upon human life in general and the eighteenth century in particular. The *Elegy* possesses the subtle appeal of flattering the reader into separating himself from the redeemed, obscurely virtuous villagers and attaching himself to the toiling bearers of power. The ultimate ironic implication of the *Elegy*, that we gladly suffer the curse of greatness in order to enjoy its fruits, is no misleading account of human nature. In the vacuous lines of the *Ode for Music*, Gray was to destroy the power of this appeal by supplying only one, deadly conventional half of the dilemma:

> What is grandeur, what is power?
> Heavier toil, superior pain.
>
> [ll. 57–58]

Reality winces at the sound. But the theme of wasted virtue, merit unrewarded, talents denied expression (at the center of the *Elegy*) echoes the cry of Swift, Fielding, and Johnson against their common society; we hear it in *Gulliver's Travels*, in *Tom Jones*, and in *London.*

There is nevertheless a sense in which *The Bard* does make a profound appeal to reality. In the final analysis Gray's contrast between impetuosity and restraint becomes identified with the meaning of the poem. The

[19] In the life of Gray.

impetuous bard, making propaganda for liberty and justice, opposes the fixed, oppressive tyrant who kills the imagination; the gushing torrent of creation streams beside the rocky, corpse-littered mountain; art confronts reality. Writing to Beattie (years after this ode appeared) and discussing the hero of *The Minstrel*, Gray recommended that when Edwin was driven to become a bard, he should perform some "great and singular service to his country." Such an action, said Gray, would constitute "the best panegyrick of our favourite and celestial science" (i.e., of poetry). There are several remarkable features in Gray's statement. One is that he could not himself specify what the sublime service might be; another is that, according to Gray, simply creating poetry is not itself enough. Yet the deed must be one requiring the peculiar talents of a poet —"some great and singular service to his country? (what service I must leave to your invention) such as no general, no statesman, no moralist could do without the aid of music, inspiration, and poetry. This will not appear an improbability in those early times, and in a character then held sacred, and respected by all nations."[20] Without telling us much about Gray that Arnold did not intimate in his essay, these remarks do point at both the source of the energy the poet poured into the ode and the cause of its failure. "In those early times" the poet's character was truly sacred; in those times he could perform services in the power of no mere general, statesman, or moralist. But now such a character would appear too improbable to admit into the design of a serious literary work. If the life of his own time represented reality, Gray clearly felt that the poet's role in it was nugatory. This is why *The Bard* never reaches out beyond the limits of literature. Just how remote Gray thought that a true poet must be, in the middle of the eighteenth century, from any deep influence upon his fellow countrymen, just how far inferior he must remain to soldiers (on the eve of the Seven Years' War and Pitt's imperial victories), to politicians, and to priests, we may infer from the conclusion of this *chef d'oeuvre*; the "celestial science" means prophesying to those who cannot understand you and then suffering martyrdom. Of course, during a regime in which devotion to literature is itself a heroic act (as in Baudelaire's France), this would be a significant relationship to one's time; but Gray's gesture belongs in a different class. The vision asserted by Collins in the *Ode on the Poetical Character*, the vision reinterpreted by Coleridge half a century later, was denied to Gray. For all its splendor *The Bard* is an assertion of its author's impotence.

The slogan of the embattled critic-scholars of the 1930s was that form is meaning. But this cry becomes serviceable only when a degree of tau-

[20] Letter of July 2, 1770—the day Gray signed his will.

tology is implied: significant form, effective structure, has a direct bearing on meaning. The corruption of the slogan by epigones produced the assumption, which underlies the unwieldy bulk of academic critical analysis, that any discussion of formal structure is, by some mysterious action at a distance, a discussion of meaning and value. Johnson's Dick Minim the critic prides himself on every instance of expressive form that he can isolate. Yet the tendency disproves itself, for surely one cannot judge the expressiveness of a verse unless one grasps the meaning of the poem, and surely the meaning depends upon a relation to reality. To pretend that there are such things as self-contained aesthetic objects or that poems are arrangements of the sounds and the lexical implications of separate words is to deny the impulse that patently drives every great artist. He is always trying to say something of immense importance to him: this is what *he* (not the poem) means; this is his "intention"; this is what we must apprehend. In every age the supreme geniuses have wished to be measured against reality, against the truths of human nature, the facts of the social order. Wordsworth said he wished to trace, in the *Lyrical Ballads*, "the primary laws of our nature"; Coleridge said the merits of *The Three Graves* were "exclusively psychological."[21] When we narrow the grounds of their achievement and judge them by a simpler standard than they themselves proposed, when we reserve for Dostoevsky and Kafka the test of reality but limit the reference of the Augustans to terms of art, I suspect we are not honoring but insulting the masters of our poetry.

[21] See the sixth paragraph of the 1800 preface and Coleridge's headnote to his poem.

V. The Styles of Gulliver's Travels

MOST SCHOLARS dealing with *Gulliver's Travels* in recent years have tried to demonstrate the structural unity or moral coherence of the book. I am not sure its appeal depends on any such quality. Henry James once said, "No themes are so human as those that reflect for us, out of the confusion of life, the close connexion of bliss and bale, of the things that help with the things that hurt."[1] It seems to me that Swift found life and human nature penetrated by polarities which only God could resolve, and that instead of transcending them, he tried to infuse them into the art of his masterpiece.

We might expect this to be so from the character of the best writing in his other works. When Swift writes well, he uses a mixed or impure style. I mean, he drops without warning from refined language into coarse language; his tone often sounds wrong for his meaning; he applies indecorous expressions to dignified subjects. For example, there is a well-known passage in the fourth *Drapier's Letter*—which he interrupted *Gulliver's Travels* to write; here Swift uses the following argument when he denounces English leaders for attacking Irish self-government:

'Tis true indeed, that within the memory of man, the parliaments of England have *sometimes* assumed the power of binding this kingdom by laws enacted there, wherein they were at first openly opposed (as far as *truth*, *reason* and *justice* are capable of *opposing*) by the famous Mr. Molineaux, an English gentleman born here, as well as by several of the greatest patriots, and *best Whigs* in England; But the *love and torrent* of power prevailed. Indeed the arguments on both sides were invincible; For in *reason*, all *government* without the consent of the *governed* is the *very definition of slavery*: But in *fact, eleven men well armed will certainly subdue one single man in his shirt.* But I have done. For those who have used *power* to cramp *liberty* have gone so far as to resent even the *liberty of complaining*, altho' a man upon the rack was never known to be refused the liberty of *roaring* as loud as he thought fit.[2]

This passage might be described as impure in style because of the author's treatment of the king. In the political rhetoric of Swift's day it was cus-

[1] Preface to *What Maisie Knew*, in Henry James, *The Art of the Novel: Critical Prefaces*, ed. R. P. Blackmur (New York: Scribner, 1934), p. 143.

[2] *The Drapier's Letters*, ed. H. Davis (Oxford: Clarendon, 1935; 2nd ed., 1965), p. 79. I ignore capitals and italics unless they have the modern meaning.

tomary to treat the king as above the battle. If the government made a mistake, the blame fell on ministers; the crown was implicitly absolved—just as in the drama of the period bad actions performed by kings had to be suggested to them by humbler men, and Dryden represented the eunuch Alexas as inventing the story of Cleopatra's suicide. But when Swift in an apparently decorous sentence says, "The love and torrent of power prevailed," he really meant that George I's own tyranny prevailed. By invoking the dignified abstractions of conventional references to royalty, he does not screen the king but accuses him.

From this elevation of language Swift sinks quickly to coarseness as he pictures a man in his shirt roaring loud upon the rack. The sudden glissando between levels of style is so arranged that the coarseness of the low image embodies the innuendo of the polished expressions. It is entirely characteristic of Swift that the fictitious elements—the single man in his shirt and on the rack—should enjoy a concrete particularity that the historical and rational elements lack. Fantasy releases Swift's concrete imagination, all the more when his tone is comic. One observes that he repeats the word "liberty" three times at this point. Here he is again indecorous. For "liberty" was a watchword of the Whig party; one expects it to be invoked by their sympathizers. But throughout the paragraph Swift the Tory is denouncing a specifically Whig policy.

At the end of the fourth *Drapier's Letter* the author discusses a scandalous rumor. According to this, the prime minister of Great Britain said he would make the Irish people swallow in fireballs the coins minted by William Wood under a royal license. The Irish were in fact wholeheartedly rejecting these coins. In order to disprove the scandalous rumor, Swift argues that Walpole is too wise a minister to talk in such a way. Then he rises to the honorific, impersonal height of language proper for allusions to the prime minister: "As his integrity is above all corruption, so is his fortune above all temptation." The true meaning of the compliment is that Walpole was celebrated for giving and taking bribes and his immense wealth was derived from immense corruption. Once again a high style is matched by a low meaning, and we taste the impurity of Swift at his best.

But directly beside the high style of this aphorism about Walpole, Swift fixed a paragraph of fantasy, bristling with concrete but imaginary particulars and implying in the coarsest way the true reason the English minister would not impose the coins on Ireland, viz., that the job would require too many soldiers:

> As to *swallowing these half-pence in fire-balls*, it is a story equally improbable. For to execute this *operation* the whole stock of Mr. Wood's coyn and metal must be melted down and molded into hollow *balls* with *wild-fire*, no bigger than a *reasonable* throat can be able to swallow. Now the metal he

hath prepared, and already coyned will amount to at least fifty millions of half-pence to be *swallowed* by a million and a half of people; so that allowing two half-pence to each *ball*, there will be about seventeen *balls* of *wild-fire* a-piece to be swallowed by every person in this kingdom, and to administer this dose, there cannot be conveniently fewer than fifty thousand *operators*, allowing one *operator* to every thirty, which, considering the *squeamishness* of some stomachs and the *peevishness* of *young children*, is but reasonable. Now, under correction of better judgments, I think the trouble and charge of such an experiment would exceed the profit, and therefore I take this *report* to be *spurious*. [pp. 86–87]

The bald juxtaposition of the low style and the high, the particular and the general, the coarse and the refined, is matched by the impurity of tone or feeling.

The feeling is impure because Swift here mixes together attitudes that one would expect him to keep separate. When the author indulges himself in so luscious a description of the fireball operation, he makes the act not ugly but captivating. His material may be ultimately and essentially repulsive; but his brisk, genial tone is sympathetic. Here is violence without pathos. Swift sounds like Voltaire, brightly summarizing Candide's disasters in the happiest voice. So energetic a world is profoundly inviting. The reader can hardly keep from representing the scene to himself in his own mind and wishing to share in it as a child wishes to share the fantasy violence of Beatrix Potter's stories. Like the celebrated remark in *A Tale of a Tub*—"Last week I saw a woman flay'd, and you will hardly believe, how much it altered her appearance for the worse"—the idea challenges our powers of aversion. Of course, after one suppresses the delight felt in the farce called up by Swift's fantasy of the fireballs, what remains is a rational statement, viz., that England cannot afford to send as many soldiers as would be needed to make the Irish accept the coins. This clearly is what the author means at bottom.

But the meaning too is impure. Repeatedly in the *Drapier's Letters* the author speaks for the ruling minority in Ireland, i.e., the Protestants descended from the English settlers. He says, "Our ancestors reduced this kingdom to the obedience of England" (p. 70). It was the self-rule of this group—or, rather, their hegemony in Ireland—that Swift wished to see restored. Why then did he appeal to the doctrine of government by consent? Why did he denounce military power as a means of establishing a tyranny? These slogans might have been exhortations to the native Roman Catholic majority to rise up and throw off their own oppressors. Swift understood perfectly that without the backing of British power his English people and his Anglican church would vanish from Ireland like hoarfrost in sunshine. Two formulations were available to him: one, a cautious style that would convey no more than he properly meant, but that would miss some of the force he wanted; the other, an outrageous expression that implied more than he deliberately intended but that exploded with violence. He gladly chose outrage and risked being misunderstood. Later in the century, both Irish and American libertarians were to use his language for the purposes it suggested, regardless of the author's original desires.

A truly scrupulous critic, who can tell a pamphleteer from a philosopher, will not agree with me. He will observe that in such passages the author seems to discourage the drawing of secondary inferences. For the author keeps returning to the peculiar condition of a specific group of people in one place during an extraordinary crisis. If he invokes general laws, he avoids any hint of a general application. But to this I reply that style works like wine; it preserves and it intoxicates. In Swift's phrasing the general proposition takes on a life independent of the local setting; and the reader, excited by a detachable aphorism, applies it as far as it can go.

One might reflect, again, that the subject of the *Drapier's Letters* is political, and Swift's disillusionment with statesmen of all colors could have driven him to take risks he did not notice. But if we look at what was nearest his heart, he will sound quite as impure. In Swift's most brilliant essay on religion, *An Argument against Abolishing Christianity*, the author considers the effect of reviving what he calls "real Christianity" and says,

> I hope, no reader imagines me so weak to stand up in the defence of *real* Christianity; such as used in primitive times (if we may believe the authors of those ages) to have an influence upon mens belief and actions: To offer at the restoring of that, would indeed be a wild project; it would be to dig up foundations; to destroy at one blow *all* the wit, and *half* the learning of the kingdom; to break the entire frame and constitution of things; to ruin trade, extinguish arts and sciences with the professors of them; in short, to turn our courts, exchanges and shops into desarts: And would be full as absurd as the proposal of Horace, where he advises the Romans, all in a body, to leave their city, and seek a new seat in some remote part of the world, by way of cure for the corruption of their manners.[3]

The style here depends on the wrongness of the tone. Not a man of God but an irreligious gentleman of fashion is what one hears in polite phrases like "I hope," in the writer's deference to the reader, in the skepticism suggested by epithets like "weak" and "absurd," in the choice of an Horatian rather than a biblical text, in the obsession with good breeding rather than virtue. It is clear from the context that this is a sort of person for whom Swift had contempt; and the passage is in fact a satirical par-

[3] *Prose Works*, ed. H. Davis (Oxford: Blackwell, 1939–68), II, 27–28.

ody of the way such men speak. The elegance of the style is a mark of corruption. Ultimately, this elegance must repel the reader, associated as it is with an indifference to morality and religion.

The immediate effect is far indeed from repulsion. Sir Fopling, in *The Man of Mode*, or Witwoud, in *The Way of the World*, could hardly please us more. One feels the writer thoroughly enjoyed acting his part, and surely one would like to act it with him. To throw off the chains of Christian conscience, to dance in the winged sandals of a pagan spirit—such invitations are hard to reject.

Suppose one did reject them? What would remain? Is the serious meaning of the passage all that interesting? Would the restoration of real Christianity "ruin trade, extinguish arts and sciences . . . turn our courts, exchanges and shops into desarts"? If it would, did Swift mean we must abandon real Christianity? If it would not, why did he make the speaker say it would? There is nothing innately false in the remark. A less witty version will be found in *The Pilgrim's Progress*: during the trial of Faithful in Vanity Fair, Envy accuses him of saying that "Christianity, and the customs of our town of Vanity, were diametrically opposite, and could not be reconciled."[4] Was Swift, like Bunyan, ringing one more change on a Gospel tune?

One could deal with these issues by referring to Swift's life, to his letters and diaries. One could show that his sermons and prayers agree with his conversations in fixing the sense of the passage from the *Argument against Abolishing Christianity*. For example, one reference of the essay certainly is to the so-called Test Act, a law according to which nobody might hold an office under the crown unless he took communion in the Established Church once a year. When people were trying (yet once more) to repeal the Test in Ireland, Swift wrote to a friend that £50,000 had been collected for the campaign. "The money," said Swift, "is sufficient among us—to abolish Christianity itself."[5] If I now state that the *Argument* is an attack on the enemies of the Test and that Swift was saying those who wished to repeal the law would have been just as glad to abolish Christianity, how much have I accomplished? The essay clearly widens the attack. In it, the local, peculiar crisis obviously stands for the grand problem of religious hypocrisy conceived in the largest terms. Could one clarify it without simplifying and reducing it? Maybe one would be wiser to leave it impure and resonant.

In *Gulliver's Travels* Part One is a nursery of such problems. When Gulliver discusses Lilliputian politics, he treats the High Heels and the Low

[4] Bunyan, *Pilgrim's Progress*, ed. J. B. Wharey, 2nd ed., rev. R. Sharrock (Oxford: Clarendon, 1960), p. 93.

[5] Nov. 20, 1733, to Charles Ford.

Heels as equally absurd. Or at least, he seems to do so. If one reads attentively, one observes that the High Heels (who stand for the Tories) are in the majority and are also "most agreeable" to the constitution of Lilliput. From these clues one might infer that the author preferred Tories to Whigs. But the preference is easy to ignore. The comic atmosphere bathing both parties leaves neither with much dignity. Certainly the playful potted history of Lilliput as told to Gulliver hardly dwells on the moral superiority of the High Heels.

The same difficulty arises with the Big-Endians and the Little-Endians. Which of the two sects is the dottier? Gulliver says that when people find it so hard to choose, the decision ought to be left to what he calls the "chief magistrate," i.e., the government. Again, if one pays strict attention, one may conclude that Gulliver speaks for the author and that Swift believed a kingdom is best off when all its subjects attend the same church; consequently, when they are confused and divided between two churches that seem equally valid, they ought to be directed to the one established by law.

The difficulty here is precisely the same as with the political issue. Gulliver's brisk, bright tone does not encourage one to treat him so seriously. The reader not only supposes that the author saw little significant distinction between reformed and unreformed churches. He also assumes that religious doctrines in general were frivolous things to him. In Part Four the reader finds this assumption confirmed. Telling the Houyhnhnms about wars fought for the sake of religion, Gulliver describes them as due to what he calls "difference in opinions," i.e., religious doctrines: "Difference in opinions hath cost many millions of lives: For instance, whether *flesh* be *bread*, or *bread* be *flesh*: Whether the juice of a certain *berry* be *blood* or *wine*: Whether *whistling* be a vice or a virtue: Whether it be better to *kiss a post*, or throw it into the fire: What is the best colour for a *coat*, whether *black*, *white*, *red* or *grey*; and whether it should be *long* or *short*, *narrow* or *wide*, *dirty* or *clean*."[6] A reader would have to be preternaturally subtle not to believe Gulliver is here the author's mouthpiece and that the author considered it absurd to trouble oneself over such matters as transubstantiation, the use of music in worship, and so forth. And what is the reader to make of the report that the Lilliputians "bury their dead with their heads directly downwards; because they hold an opinion, that in eleven thousand moons they are all to rise again; in which period, the earth (which they conceive to be flat) will turn upside down, and by this means they shall, at their resurrection, be found ready standing on their feet, (pp. 57–58). Is this the proper language to use if a man wishes his readers to maintain the Christian doctrine of the resur-

[6] *Prose Works*, XI, 246.

rection of the body? Could a man even use such language if he truly held that doctrine himself?

When the meaning of Part One of *Gulliver's Travels* does not trouble us, the tone does, for it shifts unpredictably. The Emperor of Lilliput decides to produce an unusually dignified and stirring military display. He has Gulliver stand with his legs apart like a colossus and calls for a grand parade. A general draws the troops up in close order and marches them under the giant: "the foot by twenty-four in a breast, and the horse by sixteen, with drums beating, colours flying and pikes advanced. This body consisted of three thousand foot, and a thousand horse." Awesome and magnificent, the proper entertainment of an emperor! Only it happens that some of the officers look up and see through Gulliver's torn breeches a sight that arouses, as Swift says, their "laughter and admiration" (p. 42).

If the style of Part One of *Gulliver's Travels* is considered in the largest sense—that is, as modes of discourse—it will appear to change continually and to lack any purity of structure. Chapter II is in the form of an autobiographical narrative; but near the end is inserted a long, descriptive report, by two other men, of the objects found in Gulliver's pockets. Chapter III has an expository account of court gymnastics, then several autobiographical anecdotes, and finally a treaty of nine articles, in the language of diplomacy, settling the terms on which Gulliver is to be freed. Chapter IV has a few anecdotes and then a long history of Lilliput in the form of a speech by the Secretary of State. The style of the speech is that of a political pamphlet, sober and humorless, although the events are absurd.

All through Part One of *Gulliver*, Swift carries on this variety or jumble of styles. He enjoys exhibiting his ventriloquism. He can imitate every level of style; he can take off the manners of the learned professions and reflect the spectrum of social characters. One of his happiest performances is the impeachment of Gulliver, presented in Chapter VII. Here Swift mimics the high, legal terms of the articles of impeachment drawn up against his own friends in 1715. But at the same time he ridicules those charges by the coarseness or triviality of Gulliver's details. For example, the first article, for all the euphemistic technicality of its surface, is simply about pissing in public:

> Whereas, by a statute made in the reign of his imperial majesty Calin Deffar Plune, it is enacted, that whoever shall make water within the precincts of the royal palace, shall be liable to the pains and penalties of high treason: notwithstanding, the said Quinbus Flestrin, in open breach of the said law, under colour of extinguishing the fire kindled in the apartment of his majesty's most dear imperial consort, did maliciously, traitorously, and devilishly, by discharge of his urine put out the said fire kindled in the said apartment,

lying and being within the precincts of the said royal palace; against the statute in that case provided . . . .[p. 68]

The impropriety of the action, not only in itself but in contrast to the elaboration of syntax and diction, is the basis of the satire. If the style were decorous or pure, the satire would evaporate.

This seventh chapter of Part One is in general among the most dazzling of Swift's performances. The bulk of it is a speech by one of Gulliver's friends at court. Here Swift's mastery of the flattering manner of courtiers is only the beginning of his art. The gradual revelation of what words like "friend" and "justice" mean to kings and their counselors is the end. In the following paragraph very little takes place in each sentence. A simple statement is spun out with relative clauses and adverbial phrases; the speaker pays more attention to the moral implications of the act he reports than to the act itself. The modern reader forgets a courtier is speaking and momentarily accepts his moral judgment. The reader also waits in some suspense to learn the opinion offered by Reldresal, but he assumes it will be that Gulliver deserves to go free and unpunished. When the courtier finally tells us what Reldresal advises, he conveys the message in six quick words. But Swift plants them in a conditional clause and has Reldresal rush on to the main clause, which deals with the Emperor's mercy. Thus Swift violates the decorum of syntax by which we ordinarily expect the main clause to give us a more important meaning than the subordinate clauses. Although the tempo of the paragraph seems slow, the final revelation of Reldresal's opinion is over before we can take it in; and we are left gasping while Reldresal himself proceeds to a lingering contemplation of higher things:

Upon this incident, Reldresal, Principal Secretary for Private Affairs, who always approved himself your true friend, was commanded by the Emperor to deliver his opinion, which he accordingly did; and therein justified the good thoughts you have of him. He allowed your crimes to be great; but that still there was room for mercy, the most commendable virtue in a prince, and for which his majesty was so justly celebrated. He said, the friendship between you and him was so well known to the world, that perhaps the most honourable board might think him partial: However, in obedience to the command he had received, he would freely offer his sentiments. That if his majesty, in consideration of your services, and pursuant to his own merciful disposition, would please to spare your life, and only give order to put out both your eyes; he humbly conceived, that by this expedient, justice might in some measure be satisfied, and all the world would applaud the *lenity* of the Emperor, as well as the fair and generous proceedings of those who have the honour to be his counsellors. [p. 70]

Here Gulliver is reporting a speech to us. Within that speech we hear a friendly, nameless courtier, who is trying to help Gulliver and who comments on Reldresal's speech as though it were peculiarly good-natured. Later Gulliver himself will apologize for taking another view. Not only has Swift cleverly designed the dramatic situation so that we have every reason to trust the judgment of all three men. He has also cast the paragraph in the easy, digressive, modest style that one associates with a truly good-natured man, a philanthropist. The style is therefore acutely indecorous, wholly out of keeping with the real sense of the speaker. Swift has deliberately thrust together a character and a voice that should be kept apart.

My reason for treating the style of Part One of *Gulliver* in minute detail is that it exhibits qualities not found in Part Four. For example, when Gulliver describes the Yahoos, there is no gap between the expression and the meaning. The detestation he feels for them bathes his language. He goes out of his way to pack the descriptions with epithets of disgust. "Upon the whole, I never beheld in all my travels so disagreeable an animal, or one against which I naturally conceived so strong an antipathy. So that thinking I had seen enough, full of contempt and aversion, I got up and pursued the beaten road, hoping it might direct me to the cabbin of some Indian. I had not gone far when I met one of these creatures full in my way, and coming up directly to me. The ugly monster, when he saw me, distorted several ways every feature of his visage" (p. 224). The next time Gulliver sees them, he calls them "detestable," "abominable," "filthy": "I never saw any sensitive being so detestable on all accounts; and the more I came near them, the more hateful they grew" (pp. 229–30). Elsewhere they are "odious animals" (p. 265), "filthy, noisome, and deformed," "restive and indocible, mischievous and malicious" (p. 272). It is as though we had to be warned constantly against them. Swift does not dare to give us luscious descriptions of the Yahoos or encourage us to join unconsciously in their filthy vices.[7]

But if this heavy-handedness sounds oppressive, it is also decorous and clear. One understands what the author means. Yahoos are a no-no. Swift never treated the Lilliputians this way. They were doll-like, and their coldest corruptions never frightened us. Swift let them captivate his reader and let their depravity flash forth with neither warning nor label, in the midst of their graces. The reader was inclined to dismiss their marks of vice as one tolerates rudeness in children. To use James's words, Swift suggested in Part One of *Gulliver* the "close connexion of bliss and bale."

In Houyhnhnmland, on the contrary, he exerts himself to keep the sides apart. For example, Gulliver among the Lilliputians and Brobding-

[7] Of course, there is a rhetorical reason, viz., to make Gulliver's revulsion—when he discovers the Yahoos are human—as powerful as possible.

nagians made a great to-do about feces and urine. He conspicuously emptied his bowels and bladder; he exposed his genitals; he involved his hosts in the functions of his body; he was rumored to have compromised himself sexually with a Lilliputian lady; he perched on the nipple of a Brobdingnagian maid of honor. In Part Four one would not know the Houyhnhnms ever heard of liquid or solid waste. But the Yahoos consecrate a surprising share of their leisure to the discharge of excrement. Gulliver can hardly go near them without being treated as a chamber pot or risking rape.

At the same time, Part Four allows Swift few opportunities to show off his talent for concrete, comic fantasy. Much of this part is general or abstract in tendency. The Houyhnhnms offer little for Swift to represent, because they lack the courts, exchanges and shops of European civilization. The Lilliputians have everything. Since the essence of the fantasy in Part One is to reduce natural sizes to a twelfth of what is normal, Swift can enchant us endlessly with his imaginary observations. The more general passages surveying Lilliputian manners and history make a delicious contrast because they commonly suggest parallels in real English life and thus take us not only out of the concreteness but also out of the unreality of the fantasy. But in Part Four the author denies the reader the pleasure of interpreting the parallels for himself; instead, Gulliver remorselessly spells them out. So the reader suffers page upon page of Juvenalian fury over the defects of Western culture.

As I said before, traditional decorum required poets to represent high personages, regardless of their character and deeds, in elevated language and imagery. Like many earlier satirists, Swift loved to violate or play games with this rule. In Part One the etiquette of the court and the complexities of the social structure allowed Swift to drench the story in ironies as he opposed the dignity of the courtiers to the meanness of their motives. There was no limit to the possibility of nuance. In Part Four he cannot produce such manipulations of style because if any tradition existed for describing horses and apes, it was to treat them in a low style. Unfortunately, the Houyhnhnms are seldom to be mocked; so Swift must generally treat them in straightforward language. When he does, from time to time, use the high style—for example, when the Houyhnhnm lets Gulliver lift his hoof to Gulliver's mouth at their leavetaking—the effect backfires. Instead of interpreting the passage as satire on courtiers, the modern reader is likely to see it as undercutting either Gulliver or his master.

The Yahoos, as I have said, receive only the low terms appropriate to them, in a style that is hardly interesting. Classless and chaotic, their significance can be enriched only by direct reference to general human nature—a tiresome and repetitious device. Their manners are a *reductio ad absurdum* of European manners. One cannot satirize the Yahoos; they are themselves a vehicle of satire—but a clumsy vehicle, conveying the broadest and most familiar effects in an elementary parallelism. Even this collapses at last when Swift merely identifies them with humanity.

Not much happens in Part Four. I mean, physical, visible action is far scarcer than in Part One. Gulliver cannot share the occupations of the Houyhnhnms as he shared those of the Lilliputians. His great business is talking and listening, telling his master about Europe and hearing the master's reflections. The dull plan of this voyage derives from the lack of action. Chapters IV, V, VI, and VII are a set of formal dialogues and harangues. The Houyhnhnm questions Gulliver about his own life and European society. Gulliver replies. The naive Houyhnhnm is incredulous and horror-stricken. The Houyhnhnm asks Gulliver about war. Gulliver replies. The Houyhnhnm is horrified. The Houyhnhnm asks Gulliver about law. Gulliver replies. The Houyhnhnm is horrified. After further discussions of trade, medicine, and government, Gulliver ends his course of lectures on civilization. The Houyhnhnm then lectures him on the parallels between the Yahoos and the Europeans. Gulliver is not horrified. In fact, he could not agree more. The design of these chapters—mechanical and repetitious—is typical of the whole voyage. Topics are laboriously examined; observations are made and repeated; banal inferences are drawn.

A dreary feature of Part Four is the agreement between Gulliver and the Houyhnhnm. They sing in perfect unison. When the King of Brobdingnag discussed European manners with Gulliver, the dialogue was vitalized by the antithesis between the giant's wisdom and the Englishman's fatuousness. This opposition of character matched the opposition of attitudes, since the giant was disgusted by institutions that the Englishman found unexceptionable. No such contrast relieves the tedium of the Houyhnhnm's conversations with Gulliver. It is true that the naïveté so often revealed by Gulliver in the first two voyages is transferred to the Houyhnhnm in the last, while the giant king's pessimism is transferred to Gulliver. But since both speakers have the same opinions in Part Four, the difference in their attitudes produces no drama.

The uniformity of meaning and feeling, the parallelism between sense and structure, establish a bleak uniformity of style. Just as we lose the variety of modes found earlier, so we meet certain syntactic features that make Part Four seem all of a piece. The quantity of exposition required by the dialogues on European institutions encourages Swift to go through subjects in lists and categories—to cover them, as it were. He is addicted, in Part Four, to sentences made of a series of substantive clauses introduced by the conjunction *that*. This habit derives naturally from the burdensome use of indirect discourse:

I made his honour my most humble acknowledgements for the good opinion he was pleased to conceive of me; but assured him at the same time, *that* my birth was of the lower sort, having been born of plain, honest parents, who were just able to give me a tolerable education; *that*, nobility among us was altogether a different thing from the idea he had of it; *that*, our young noblemen are bred from their childhood in idleness and luxury; *that*, as soon as years will permit, they consume their vigour, and contract odious diseases among lewd females; and when their fortunes are almost ruined, they marry some woman of mean birth, disagreeable person, and unsound constitution, merely for the sake of money, whom they hate and despise. *That*, the productions of such marriages are generally scrophulous, rickety or deformed children; by which means the family seldom continues above three generations, unless the wife take care to provide a healthy father among her neighbours, or domesticks, in order to improve and continue the breed. *That*, a weak diseased body, a meager countenance, and sallow complexion, are the true marks of *noble blood*. [pp. 256–57—my italics]

When Swift is writing carefully, he does not allow himself to tumble half a dozen such members together and offer the disjointed carcase as a live sentence. The whole of Part One yields up two sentences with three such clauses and two with four.

When the sentences are not so cumbersome in form, Swift still overloads them with enumerations of items or chains of phrases; e.g., the Houyhnhnm discovers that Gulliver "differed very much from the rest of my species, in the whiteness, and smoothness of my skin, my want of hair in several parts of my body, the shape and shortness of my claws behind and before, and my affectation of walking continually on my two hinder feet" (p. 237). Compare this enumeration of five points with Gulliver's description of the Emperor of Lilliput, in which Swift exerts himself to avoid a mere listing of attributes. Notice there how he shifts his verbs from "was" to "had" to "held," while changing the subject of the verb from "he" to "I" and mixing observation with action in the phrases of description—and reflect that he does all this in order to keep the portrait interesting as a bit of prose: "His dress was very plain and simple, the fashion of it between the Asiatick and the European; but he had on his head a light helmet of gold, adorned with jewels, and a plume on the crest. He held his sword drawn in his hand, to defend himself, if I should happen to break loose; it was almost three inches long, the hilt and scabbard were gold enriched with diamonds. His voice was shrill, but very clear and articulate, and I could distinctly hear it when I stood up" (pp. 30–31). Descriptions based on mere enumeration will be found in Lilliput, but not often. In Houyhnhnmland they are the rule.

Still worse is the tendency to compile catalogues of epithets and creatures in Part Four. I must point out that Swift sometimes used what might be called a mock-catalogue for ironical effects. Thus praising the serenity of his life in Houyhnhnmland, Gulliver says the country has "no lords, fidlers, judges, or dancing-masters" (p. 277). Unfortunately, this is the only passage of Part Four in which Swift used the device. Homogeneous catalogues of the most banal sort are frequent and normal. There are half a dozen of these in the last chapter alone. Here is a catalogue of elements of war, from Chapter V: "I gave him a description of cannons, culverins, muskets, carabines, pistols, bullets, powder, swords, bayonets, sieges, retreats, attacks, undermines, countermines, bombardments, sea-fights" (p. 247). Here is a catalogue of elements of marriage, which the Houyhnhnms flourish without, taken from Chapter VIII: "Courtship, love, presents, joyntures, settlements, have no place in their thoughts" (p. 269). The whole of Part One has only five of these catalogues.

I know very well how my complaints against Part Four may be dealt with. Modern criticism is not so clumsy that it cannot dispose of the judgment that a poem is badly written. There are two approved techniques for smothering literary faultfinders. First, one says the author meant to do what he did. Second, one says the style is mimetic or expressive, and it peculiarly suits the meaning.

It would be easy to argue that Swift intended to organize Part Four as a thoroughly polarized situation in which the vicious have nothing to do with the virtuous. We may speculate that the word *human*, when divided into its consonants and vowels, produces the *hnm* of "Houyhnhnm" and the *a-u* of "Yahoo"; and if so, the very names of the two races imply that the author deliberately chose to make them separate and incompatible, as an allegorical apartheid.[8]

Besides, the force of Part Four depends on its relation to the earlier parts. For three-quarters of *Gulliver's Travels* the narrator is woodenly resistant to the truths of human depravity. In Part Four at last the reader feels continually satisfied to see Gulliver's character pulled inside out, to hear him finally accepting and propagating the judgments he fought against all through his earlier voyages. In the same way it seems proper that Swift should now reverse the rhetorical pattern of *Lilliput* and, instead of mingling vice with virtue, keep them distinct. The dialogues and harangues, the cumulative sentences and the catalogues, may also reflect the author's wish to be perfectly clear. In the bitterest division of his work, where he has the most frightening doctrine to teach, he dare not risk being misunderstood. Through the simple modes of catechism, exposition, and lists, he exhausts and unmistakably expounds his lesson.

The mimetic or expressive side of Swift's style in Part Four is also easy to appreciate. Auerbach, discussing Augustine's use of parataxis, says

[8] Cf. the discussion of vowels and consonants in Swift's *Proposal for Correcting the English Tongue*, in *Prose Works*, IV, 11–13.

"The urgently impulsive element in his character makes it impossible for him to accommodate himself to the comparatively cool and rational procedure of the classical, and specifically of the Roman, style, which looks at and organizes things from above."[9] We may apply the same analysis to Gulliver in Part Four. A frenzy clutches him. He has no time to shape his periods. The principles he must put forth concerning the corruptions of mankind are not the sort to be measured out in regulated phrases. Gulliver's lists and catalogues burst from him like a barrage from a machine gun—as when he describes the advantages of living in Houyhnhnmland:

> Here was neither physician to destroy my body, nor lawyer to ruin my fortune: no informer to watch my words and actions, or forge accusations against me for hire: Here were no gibers, censurers, backbiters, pickpockets, highwaymen, house-breakers, attorneys, bawds, buffoons, gamesters, politicians, wits, spleneticks, tedious talkers, controvertists, ravishers, murderers, robbers, virtuoso's; no leaders or followers of party and faction; no encouragers to vice, by seducement or examples: no dungeon, axes, gibbets, whipping-posts, or pillories; no cheating shopkeepers or mechanicks: no pride, vanity or affectation: no fops, bullies, drunkards, strolling whores, or poxes: no ranting, lewd, expensive wives: no stupid, proud pedants: no importunate, over-bearing, quarrelsome, noisy, roaring, empty, conceited, swearing companions: no scoundrels raised from the dust upon the merit of their vices; or nobility thrown into it on account of their virtues. [pp. 276–77]

Here are the violence, the careless rage that Swift vented in typical passages of other works. Only here they break forth as the style explodes. There is no comic fantasy. There is no contrast between syntax and meaning. All is one plain invective. If such a sequence is delivered with care by a sympathetic speaker, it makes a memorable impression. I admit, therefore, the appeal of arguments commending Swift's procedures in Part Four.

But at the same time I do not see how they can change my judgment. If Swift consciously decided to grind the prose of Part Four between asyndeton above and parataxis below, so much the worse for him. If the style is expressive, it is coarsely expressive, sacrificing the nuance and subtlety of Part One to a hammering blatancy. The impression made is hardly the sort one would choose to revive. After a few paragraphs it grows boring.

Compare it with the paragraph in Part Two where the same judgment is being passed by the King of Brobdingnag. The giant uses a vocabulary that is dignified and decorous, but his sentences grow in relaxed, additive series of clauses; their structure loosens up:

> My little friend Grildrig; you have made a most admirable panegyrick upon your country. You have clearly proved that ignorance, idleness, and vice are

[9] Erich Auerbach, *Mimesis* (New York: Doubleday, 1957), p. 62.

the proper ingredients for qualifying a legislator. That laws are best explained, interpreted, and applied by those whose interest and abilities lie in perverting, confounding, and eluding them. I observe among you some lines of an institution, which in its original might have been tolerable; but these half erased, and the rest wholly blurred and blotted by corruptions. It doth not appear from all you have said, how any one perfection is required towards the procurement of any one station among you; much less that men are ennobled on account of their virtue, that priests are advanced for their piety or learning . . . or counsellors for their wisdom. [p. 132]

The combination of decorous language and loose structure survives until the last sentence, where regal refinement will give way suddenly to low, coarse invective. Yet the structure of the last sentence is almost periodic. It will have an element of suspense, a connectedness, that the others lack: "As for yourself (continued the king) who have spent the greatest part of your life in travelling; I am well disposed to hope you may hitherto have escaped many vices of your country. But, by what I have gathered from your own relation, and the answers I have with much pains wringed and extorted from you; I cannot but conclude the bulk of your natives, to be the most pernicious race of little odious vermin that nature ever suffered to crawl upon the surface of the earth" (p. 132). This is the most shapely sentence in the paragraph; it straggles least; it alone rises in intensity as it proceeds, and ends with an emotional peak. Thus as he shifts from decorous to coarse language, Swift also shifts from loose to tight construction. In the way of style nothing so seductive will be found in Part Four.

I do not mean to deny the power or profundity of Part Four. But I doubt that they spring from literary technique. At this point I should like to turn from Swift's art to his life, because what staggers us in Part Four is, I think, the cruel simplicity of the author's insight. Reading those chapters of *Gulliver's Travels*, we share with Swift a knowledge of the real bestiality into which human nature plunges when stripped of moral intelligence. Behind the Yahoo stands Caliban, whom we "do not love to look on" (*Tempest* I.ii.310). It is the monster whose reality men never like to acknowledge because it takes men, improving on nature, to produce it. The Yahoo and Caliban do not refer to the happy farmer whose healthful toil begets sweet rest at night and innocent tranquillity in sunshine. They refer to the brutalized, half-starved serf, neglected and oppressed, whose ordeal does not refine but unmans him. Only by a concerted effort can a nation's institutions destroy in numbers of people the spirit needful for a rational existence.

I suspect that Swift balanced the fantasy of Part One with the reality of Part Four. No one who looks honestly at the varieties of human condition within five miles of his backdoor can fail to observe that Yahoos are systematically fostered by the institutions on which our culture rests. The note of frenzy in Swift's voice throughout Part Four was, I think, his response to what he saw in Ireland: the dehumanized natives collaborating in their own ruin, the rulers of the kingdom blinding themselves to the nightmares they created. About Ireland Swift once wrote, "[I often examine] as I pass the streets whether those animals which come in my way with two legs and human faces, clad, and erect, be of the same species with what I have seen very like them in England, as to the outward shape, but differing in their notions, natures, and intellectualls more than any two kinds of brutes in a forest."[10] An Englishman who came over to Ireland in 1718 to be Bishop of Derry wrote that he had

> never beheld even in Picardy, Westphalia, or Scotland such dismal marks of hunger and want as appear'd in the countenances of most of the poor creatures that I met with on the road. The wretches live in reeky sod-hovels; and have generally no more than a rag of coarse blanket to cover a small part of their nakedness. Upon the strictest inquiry I could not find that they are better clad or lodg'd in the winter season. These sorry slaves plow the ground, to the very top of their mountains, for the service of their lords; who spend the (truely rack) rents . . . in London. A ridge or two of potatoes is all the poor tenant has for the support of himself, a wife, and (commonly) ten or twelve bare-legg'd children. To compleat their misery, these animals are bigotted Papists; and we frequently met them trudging to some ruin'd church or chapel, either to mass, a funeral, or a wedding, with a priest in the same habit with themselves.[11]

I think we respond sympathetically to Part Four insofar as we have learned elsewhere what Swift learned in Ireland. It is only since the Second World War that Gulliver's last voyage has held the imagination of critics, and it is only since then that we have had the irrefutable evidence of modern man's bestiality, in Germany, Russia, South Africa, and Southeast Asia. Once we accept that banality, we can take the thesis of Part Four for granted and enjoy the literary art of Part One.

[10] *Prose Works*, XII, 65.

[11] William Nicolson to William Wake, Gilbert MSS. 27, pp. 178–80, Dublin Public Library.

Index

Index